THE *10*-SECOND
INTERNET MAN@GER

THE 10-SECOND INTERNET MAN@GER

Survive, Thrive & Drive Your Company in the Information Age

MARK BREIER

with Armin A. Brott

CROWN
BUSINESS
NEW YORK

Published by Crown Business, New York, New York. Member of the Crown Publishing Group.

Random House, Inc. New York, Toronto, London, Sydney, Auckland
www.randomhouse.com

Crown Business and colophon are trademarks of
Random House, Inc.

Printed in the United States of America

Design by Barbara Sturman

Library of Congress Cataloging-in-Publication Data
Breier, Mark.
    The 10-second Internet manager/Mark Breier with Armin
Brott.—1st ed.
        p.   cm.
    1. Electronic commerce—Management.   2. Management.
3. Time management.   4. Internet (Computer network)
I. Title: 10-second Internet manager.   II. Brott, Armin A.
III. Title.
HF5548.32 .B74 2000
658′.05467—dc21   00-20814

ISBN 0-609-60732-4

10 9 8 7 6 5 4 3 2 1

First Edition

I would like to dedicate this book to:

My parents, John and Marian Breier, who gave me the
key Internet skills of practicality, people skills, humor, and
creativity;

My wife, Ronda, who energizes me daily with passion, humor,
happiness, and beauty;

My sons, Corey and Travis, who provide daily fun in racing,
wrestling, and reading;

My key business mentors Tyler Johnston, Betsy Holden,
Ed Franczek, Rick Cronk, and Gary Rogers;

And to two Internet innovators: Jeff Bezos, who invited
me into his .com inspiration (and to our mutual love of
broomball); and Bill McKiernan, who pursued me across the
border (and to our Mexican margaritas).

I would like to offer special thanks to Edie Felice Barry for
her early book inspiration and naming; to Jim Levine, my
agent, who shared the vision of doing this book in "Internet
time"; to Armin Brott, who patiently drew out experiences
and learnings from me and dozens of other busy CEOs; to
Mary Hain, who helped bring the whole project together; and
to Bonnie Savage, the world's best executive assistant, for
maintaining calm, professionalism, and efficiency amidst the
Internet tornado.

—MB

To Tirzah and Talya, who've grown up in the Internet age and
have seen typewriters and record players only in museums.

—AB

CONTENTS

Everyone wants to know the secret. Strangers at industry con-
ventions, recruiters from Fortune 500 companies, entrepreneurs via e-mail, phone calls, Fed Ex, and fax. And what do
they want? They want the secret sauce of the Internet, the
road map to personal success, riches, and fame.

Well, I know a little bit about that secret. You see, I
have ridden the waves of Internet fame and fortune the last
four years.

First, at Amazon.com, which I joined four months before
it went public, when most people had not heard about it. As
vice president of marketing, I helped develop funny radio ads
(is the Pentagon big enough for Amazon.com's books? the
Rose Bowl?), launched innovative promotions (want to write
a book with John Updike?), and participated in the company's
hypergrowth as it zoomed past one million customers and one
thousand employees.

And more recently as president and CEO at Beyond.com,
where, in just one year, I helped make it one of the top ten

e-commerce sites, helped propel it to a market capitalization of over $1 billion, and obtained $250 million in financing for its war chest. But as quickly as the wave arrived, it receded. Investors moved from business to consumer (B2C) enthusiasm to a business to business (B2B) trend. In the second year, I transformed the company to a B2B company, building upon Beyond.com's past success in selling software to the government and to running websites for software publishers.

Today, I make a career out of advising and investing in Internet start-ups. It's a worthy cause. After all, the Internet is about building a better world via increased communication, greater convenience, improved information access, and personal empowerment.

I invite you to participate in that cause. Visit *www.10 secondmanager.com* to find more tips from industry leaders, influencers, and me and add your own insights to the discussion.

INTRODUCTION

I do everything fast. I think fast. I talk fast. I play fast. I make decisions fast. I always have. Then I came to work in and run an Internet company, the fastest—and fastest-changing—thing around. That meant I had to hire fast, buy companies fast, change strategies fast, put out fires fast, and push people to do things they never thought they could—and to do them faster than they ever could have dreamed.

When I was first out of college, I remember picking up a book called *The One Minute Manager.* I liked it a lot. I was running my own business, a party- and event-planning company called Amazing Events. We did things like arrange for a chorus of tap-dancing pickles to greet the U.S.S. *Coral Sea,* courtesy of the admiral's wife. Or, as a corporate party gag, chip a golf ball into a board meeting, then send a golfer, a caddy, a television announcer, and a course marshal in after it.

But back to *The One Minute Manager.* I was really impressed with the book's simple, commonsense approach (and given its enduring sales record, I'm clearly not alone). Over the years I've recommended the book to lots of people. But recently I was telling a colleague about it when I suddenly realized I'd completely forgotten the details of the book's message. I could still remember the main points: that managers can and should act quickly and at the same time value their people. But the subtleties had faded from my memory. I decided to reread the book.

I ordered a copy and enjoyed a pleasant surge of nostalgia as I held the familiar, compact volume in my hand. But within minutes of starting to read, I found myself getting incredibly impatient at the author's leisurely stroll through the book's key points. Frustrated, I put the book down. Working in the Internet world had so completely rewired my mind that I'd actually believed *The One Minute Manager* was a book I could read in one minute. The problem, I realized, is that the way things are going these days, it's hard for me to find a free minute.

Internet companies expand at a mind-boggling pace. They're full of super-motivated people who generate three times as many ideas as any company could possibly handle. Internet customers demand more and better and faster every single day, and companies are trying to build and maintain a technology war chest in a world where technology is a moving target, evolving every day.

I also didn't have a free minute because I would get dozens of calls, e-mails, letters, and requests every hour: old friends would see me interviewed on television and want to get together; there were invitations to attend Internet conferences and trade association meetings; businessmen from China were coming through town and top media executives supposedly wanted to thank me for advertising on their networks but really just wanted to pick my brain about what is all this Internet stuff anyway? I would get a half-dozen calls a month from someone who wanted to buy us or wanted us to buy them, and it would be impolite of me not to speak with

CEOs running Fortune 500–size companies who were gnashing their molars into powder over Internet stock market valuations. And then, of course, there were the reporters, politicians, nonprofit groups, and business school students who wanted to set up interviews.

Sometimes they wanted juicy insights about Amazon.com, where I used to be vice president of marketing. Sometimes they wanted feedback on the deal du jour making the headlines that had to do with Internet stocks or software wars. But the majority of the time they would want to know: What's the secret of being an Internet CEO? What's the Internet going to look like in six months? How can they get a copy of the secret to-do list that will enable them to finally jump off the Old Economy steamer and kick up some spray in an I-way speedboat? In short, they wanted to know where they can get some magic dust. You know, the stuff you add water to, stir, and—*poof!*—you've got a popular Internet company.

Believe me, if I could give them some, I'd do it in a heartbeat; it would save me a lot of time. But starting and running a successful Internet company isn't about secret lists or magic dust. The new economy requires new skills and new mind-sets. At the same time, though, the stunning successes of Amazon.com, eBay, AOL, and others were based on classic business execution: caring about customers, serving needs, and building brand loyalty. The difference is that it all has to happen at warp speed.

So here's a nice, thin book—the closest thing I have to magic dust—about what I've learned in my years of running full-throttle in the fast lane of the I-way. It's a road, sadly, where my old friend *The One Minute Manager* would probably be found facedown with tire tracks up his back. It's a fate the book certainly doesn't deserve: I agree completely that the best minute a manager can spend is with people. But what do you do when you don't have a free minute? That's why you need to learn to be *The 10-Second Internet Manager.*

In truth, we really could have left "Internet" out of the title and called this *The 10-Second Manager.* Industry evangelists are fond of saying lately that success in business isn't about being the smartest or having the best technology (although that certainly won't hurt). More than ever before, success is about speed. It's about thriving in a world where things are changing at the speed of light. And that rule applies to *every* business. So whether you're running a company that's based in cyberspace or firmly anchored in bricks and mortar, or whether you're about to go public or you're the head of the PTA at your kids' school, *The 10-Second Internet Manager* will give you the tools you need to act smart *and* act fast.

THE MAGIC DUST

Here's what *The 10-Second Internet Manager* will teach you. If you don't have time to read the rest of this introduction, just read the stuff in boldface.

1.   **Act fast and act smart.** Your edge against bigger and better-funded competitors is speed. Use it or lose everything. If you're going to do this, though, you're going to have to learn to "will" your company forward, shaving time off every task possible.

2.   **E-mail morning, noon, and night. Talk in between.** E-mail is the oxygen of the Internet. But used badly, it can smother recipients and slow down an entire company. Using e-mail effectively is what separates the savvy manager from those who don't get it.

3.   **Make feedback your friend.** The biggest problems most businesses suffer are from not listening to customers, not focusing on customer service, and not working hard to understand what customers want. Appreciating customers is one of the secrets to marketing success—whether on the Internet or anywhere else. The Internet offers tremendous opportunities to solicit and receive customer feedback. But ignoring it opens the doors to faster-moving, customer-focused outfits who will eat your lunch.

4. **Make your meetings effective.** Meetings are the bane of many employees' work lives: too much time, too much discussion and not enough action, too little respect, too much finger-pointing, too many late arrivers, and too many people who talk too much and don't stick to the point. No manager who wants to succeed in the Internet age can afford this kind of dead-end meeting.

5. **Make your brand matter.** Building a consistent, recognizable brand image on the Internet is crucial. And creating and securing a brand identity starts with the business proposition itself. To become the authority, the go-to, the "verb" for your category, every decision has to be made with brand in mind.

6. **Survive in the investment jungle.** Internet CEOs are constantly going through the ritual of pitching to investors who have the power to add and subtract billions to the company's valuation. To succeed in the Internet world you have to know how to deal with the fleecers, the youngsters, the cynics, and the investment gods.

7. **Have fun.** Work should be fun, rewarding, and empowering. But over time, obsessed workaholics will burn out. So subdivide your company into impassioned teams, celebrate successes frequently, and build a "work hard, play hard" culture. You'll reap major benefits in energy, creativity, and productivity.

The tips you'll see in each chapter are just the beginning! Visit *www.10secondmanager.com* to see more tips on how to succeed in the Information Age. Share your own insights with fellow readers.

THE SECRETS OF ACTING FAST

You can hardly walk down a street in Silicon Valley without hearing someone talking about "Internet time." A day is a week and a week is a month, they say. And a month is a year. It's a "24/7" kind of world: if you're not moving forward twenty-four hours a day, seven days a week, you're falling behind. "Internet time" not only means doing business fast but doing it anytime the customer wants and for as long as he wants it. This is what customers are demanding and it's what every Internet company is trying to offer. The result is a business culture that's always working, always aware that the perfect opportunity could come at any time, and if you're a player, you're never far away from your beeper, fax machine, e-mail, or cell phone.

I believe the pace will slow down in a few years. Right now, though, the opportunities to both create entirely new business models—like eBay—and to shake up and displace old, established businesses—as Amazon.com did to booksellers—are so big that it's almost hard to grasp. And the oil that keeps the machinery of progress moving is speed.

You may have a great business plan and a top-notch team. Or you may be running a multinational corporation with money to burn and a mandate to buy your way onto the 'Net. But that's no guarantee you'll succeed. In today's world, it's not the survival of the fittest anymore. It's survival of the fastest. As John Chambers of Cisco Systems says, "Companies will either be fast—or they'll disappear."

Let me tell you a story about just how important moving quickly can be.

In spring 1998, I had been VP of marketing for Amazon.com for over a year and my wife and I were poised to escape the Internet tornado for a week in Mexico. It had been an amazing year. In the first quarter of 1997, we had revenues of $16 million—as much business as we'd done in *all* of 1996. We were growing at 25 percent a month and revenues for the first quarter of 1998 were running at an annualized rate of $150 million. We'd developed a national radio advertising campaign that has become a model for the new, hip, funny Internet advertising that most Internet companies still can't match. One of our best was a mock quest of our people to try to find a place big enough to put the Earth's Biggest Bookstore. Maybe the Rose Bowl, the Pentagon, a Boeing aircraft hangar. Our stock was exploding and I'd hired over forty people into the marketing department. Amazon.com had been like a rocket ship for the whole year.

Long, exhausting days were common. Weekends were just two more days to work. And breaks were few and far between. Jeff Bezos, Amazon's CEO, drove his employees relentlessly forward, constantly adding new projects and new challenges. Signs of strain were everywhere. Many youthful complexions had gone pale and many people had gained weight.

In Japan there's a recognized medical condition—*karoshi*

—that means "to work yourself to death." That wasn't my work style, nor was it the one I wanted to foster in my department. Our pace was fast and often furious, but fundamentally fun. I told Jeff that giving people a chance to balance their lives a little would be good for business; they'd be more productive and happier to be working here. Jeff didn't agree. "At most companies people either work hard or fast or smart," he insisted. "But around here you've got to do all three, and that doesn't leave time for anything else."

Fortunately, I'm a pretty upbeat kind of guy, and my wife, Ronda, and I were ready to celebrate. This was going to be a rare vacation without kids. But the day before we were set to leave, I got a call from Michael Reich, a recruiter who was anxious to find a CEO for a privately held company called Software.net, an on-line seller of physical and digital software for PCs. I told him that he couldn't afford me: my Amazon stock options were skyrocketing and I wasn't about to give them up lightly. And on top of that, I didn't want to leave Amazon. So I said no.

Michael said he represented Paul Allen, Microsoft's cofounder and a major investor in Software.net, and I felt this would be a good connection to nurture. So I agreed to meet Michael briefly at Starbuck's the next morning before I got on the plane for Mexico. Surprisingly, it was a good meeting. I'd done some research at Amazon about new product categories and current industry leaders and was impressed with Software.net, particularly its dominance in digital downloading and its large government contracts. But I was headed off for vacation, so I said "thanks" and told Michael that we'd have to do any follow-up when I got back. I raced home, picked up Ronda, and we left for the airport.

We were checking in at the gate when my cell phone rang. It was Michael Reich again. "Don't get on the plane," he said. "Mr. Allen has made one of his 757s available. It's fueled, it's got a crew, and it's waiting for you at Boeing Field." It was all very simple, Michael explained. The 757 would take us from Seattle to San Jose where it would pick up Bill McKiernan, Software.net's chairman. It would then take us on to Mexico for our vacation. McKiernan and I would have a chance to talk on the plane.

Struggling to keep my face straight and my jaw off the airport floor, I looked over at Ronda, who was standing at the gate, and mouthed "Hold on a minute." The offer was so incredible—a personal 757—that it was beyond comprehension. I couldn't even put together a response.

"No can do," I told Michael. "There are only a few laws of travel, and one of them is to follow your luggage!"

Ronda and I got on the plane, laughing at the craziness of what had just happened, and we were off on our vacation. While changing planes in Los Angeles, my cell phone rang again. It was the recruiter. Bill McKiernan had hopped on a plane from San Jose, would meet us momentarily in Los Angeles and would fly with us to Cabo San Lucas! I turned to Ronda. "These guys are nuts," I said. We got on the plane and I took out an Amazon.com bookmark and stuck it in the tray table slot in front of me so McKiernan would be able to spot us if he happened to be cruising the aisles. I settled into my seat and went to sleep.

We landed in Mexico and McKiernan hadn't shown up. We laughed at how oddly things had been going but decided we were going to have a great vacation anyway. So we went to the hotel, checked in, then went out to dinner and started relaxing. But when we got back to the hotel at midnight, things began to change.

A bellhop grabbed me and pointed across the lobby to a guy in a Hawaiian shirt, shorts, and sandals who had been waiting anxiously for us. It was Bill McKiernan, of course. Turns out he'd walked right by us in the terminal in L.A. and again on the plane because he was told to look for a tall, bearded man (I'm clean-shaven).

Bill and I grabbed a couple of beers and went for a walk on the beach. He explained that in three years he'd created a company that investment bankers had told him was worth over $300 million and could grow even more. "I'm sitting on a gold mine," he said. "But I'm not the guy to run it. You are." Bill is genuine, persistent, and street-smart. Intellectually and viscerally I knew I could work with him.

For the next few weeks I was on a whirlwind interview schedule, zipping onto private jets after putting in a full day at Amazon, going to Silicon Valley to negotiate my contract, arriving back in Seattle at night so I could be back at Amazon first thing in the morning. The more time I spent with the people at Software.net, the more I liked them. They had a clear idea of where they wanted to go. They acted smart and they acted fast. Very fast.

FAST ISN'T ENOUGH . . .

At this point you may be thinking that I have an ego the size of Milwaukee. But I didn't tell you this story because I think I'm so incredibly special. If you let your ego take you down that path (and lots of Silicon Valley folks do), you're doomed. The point is that people who keep their eyes on a goal and act quickly to achieve it often find ways around the obstacles most people consider insurmountable. You can't wait for the perfect pitch or spend weeks making plans. If your company can't move forward because you need a CEO to lead it, identify some candidates fast. When you've picked the best one, land him fast. As an advisor and investor in Internet start-ups, I hear from a dozen entrepreneurs a week who are seeking to reinvent the world in ways that you and I had not previously imagined. Yet the established brick-and-mortar companies are still struggling.

What it all comes down to is what B-school types call a "bias toward action" or "avoiding analysis paralysis." It's not that the traditional businesses can't do the things many of us are doing on the Internet. It's just that they suffer from what I call the 3 Cs.

▷   **Culture.** Their cultures are too resistant; they're slow-moving and risk-averse. Most can't change because of the way they are currently organized. In some cases traditional businesses act smart, but they don't act quickly. They hire management consultants, convene large committees, produce fifty-page presentations, and do extensive risk- and break-even analyses. While Barnes & Noble and Borders were fine-tuning their reports, Amazon.com was launching a hugely successful business, getting a huge amount of publicity, and gaining mind share. Amazon.com launched in July 1996; Barnesand Noble.com didn't launch until May 1997, and Borders.com was even farther behind.

▷   **Channel conflict.** For most companies, 100 percent of their current business is threatened by Internet growth. For years, they have sold products and services using tried-and-true channels, such as retail stores, distributors, resellers, or a direct sales force. The Internet cannibalizes those channels. Theoretically, Compaq can do everything Dell is doing. But, practically, it would be very risky for Compaq to do anything that would jeopardize its retail channels. In the end, because managers find it difficult to destroy themselves, savvy competitors do it for them.

In other cases speed isn't the problem; clear thinking is. They act fast but they don't act smart. You don't, for example, take a guy whose whole bonus plan is based on how many brick-and-mortar stores report to him and how much volume those stores generate, and put him in charge of exploring Internet retailing. It would be like hiring a wolf to guard the henhouse: one of the goals of an Internet company is to take business away from physical stores. He won't want to succeed because that success would cost him money. And many traditional companies make the mistake of putting their e-commerce operations under the control of the information technology department, people who know nothing about marketing. They may build you a website, but they won't know how to move the product.

> ▷ **Compensation.** Talented managers, a requirement for success, will flow to companies that reward their performance, through a combination of salary and stock options that will vest in a public offering. Talent will not flow to companies that can't set up stand-alone companies that offer stock options and IPO prospects.

The last two Cs are examples of the hundreds of painful, don't-get-it moves that are draining millions from the bottom lines of potential players who have all the infrastructure and cash they need to play the game. This book can help managers deal with the first of these 3 Cs, the right culture. But only the boldest of CEOs and boards can make the aggressive moves needed to address the other two Cs, channel conflict and compensation, and set up a vibrant, independent organization that is the sister company's biggest competitor.

One of the best examples of acting fast and acting smart on the Internet happened right before my eyes when I was still at Amazon. Jeff Bezos is probably in the top 1 percent of people in the universe when it comes to bias toward action. He's also, without a doubt, one of the most intense people I've ever met. I've watched him conduct marathon negotiations that are more like prisoner-of-war interrogations, designed to break the will of the other party. And I've watched him organize a battle plan that would rival the Allies' preparation before the invasion of Normandy.

In the first half of 1997, over the course of ten days,

Amazon launched a series of lightning-fast, midnight attacks that enabled it to secure beachheads at the three major Internet portal sites: AOL, Yahoo!, and Excite. It was truly a thing of beauty.

Jeff had set up a few ingenious environmental rules designed to swing the negotiations in our favor. He invited our potential partners into a conference room with the intention of not letting anyone leave until a deal was made. And he timed the meetings to coincide with the portals' fiscal-quarter end, when they'd be hungriest for new partners and new sources of revenue. (Like all public companies, they issue quarterly financial reports, and they're always looking to wow the investment community with big news items on major deals. Good news does nice things to your stock price.) The rules were far from scientific and the meetings were often like bumbling, groping first dates in which neither side knew how best to proceed; still, Jeff's intensity and sense of urgency managed to keep things moving.

At one point, though, after seven deadlocked hours with AOL, we were still millions of dollars apart. Negotiations were about to break down when Jeff had an inspiration. "I'll pay your high fees if you put a 'search for (this topic) at the Amazon.com' link on every search conducted on the portal site," he offered. Since this was unsold real estate at AOL at the time, Jeff's suggestion was an innovative compromise point, and we closed the deal. He then turned around and signed agreements with Excite and Yahoo! with very similar terms and announced all of them quickly—and together. Each partner was furious. None of them had known that they were being two-timed (three-timed?).

By acting smart and fast, Jeff had put together what was, arguably, one of the most valuable deals in Internet history. In addition, the terms of the deals, including the amounts paid and the icon links (which would be "context sensitive"—based on what people were searching for), changed the face of the

Internet forever. They instantly established portals as major ad business and made portal partnership a de rigueur part of going public for all future Internet companies.

Acting fast and acting smart also resulted in a huge marketing miracle: Amazon.com got the message out (on just about every single Internet search) that it alone had a book on virtually any topic you could search for. Whether it actually did or not wasn't important, and there's been some amusing fallout. If you search for some idiosyncratic thing on one of these search engines, you'll still get a cheery splash from Amazon inviting you over to "search for books on 342 S. Main St., Apt. 8" or books on "treating dalmatian tick allergies." But none of that matters. The message is still there: Amazon.com has a book on absolutely everything.

THE SECRETS OF ACTING FAST. AND SMART.

So how does a company go about building a fast-acting, smart-acting culture? Here are some tips to help you get started:

1.   **Hire fast people.** At Beyond.com we expanded to four hundred employees in our first year, up from seventy. That may sound great, but size often breeds slowness. To avoid getting crushed under your own weight, it's crucial to hire fast people. It doesn't matter what industry they come from—the Internet is too young to demand industry experience from everyone. (Before I joined Amazon, I'd been working in food marketing for such companies as Kraft Foods, Dreyer's/Edy's Grand Ice Cream, and Cinnabon World Famous Cinnamon Rolls.) Just make sure the people you hire have four key attributes:

> ▷   A fast mind
> ▷   A bias for action
> ▷   Impatience
> ▷   Limitless energy

The hours, the stress, and the unrelenting nature of the Internet can sap the strength from a normal human being in no time. But fast, energetic people have a way of reinvigorating and motivating others. In late 1999, Beyond.com had a major site outage (meaning that thousands of frustrated customers were turned away while we retooled our database so we could handle more traffic). It was a pretty gloomy time around the office and morale was suffering. But I had four incredibly buoyant people working for me, and they were able to reenergize and inspire their departments and get their employees back on track, thinking positively, and pulling together. For some people, a site outage is practically the end of the world. But these four turned it upside down: "There are a billion websites out there and they're all begging for traffic," they said. "But we have more than we can possibly handle. We've joined e-Bay, Amazon.com, and AOL. What a great problem to have!"

So how do you find people with the qualities you need?

Look for people who tap their pencils and bounce their knees during the interview, people who look as if they just can't wait to get to work. John Doerr, the venture capitalist legend behind Sun, Amazon.com, MarthaStewart.com, and many others, is in constant motion in board meetings, fidgeting and wandering around.

Do *not* hire anyone you think would be comfortable in a four-hour meeting. The fastest person I ever worked with is Trinka Dyer, a star employee of mine at Dreyer's/Edy's Grand Ice Cream and at Beyond.com. She hates—practically goes into fits—if anything stays on her to-do list for more than twenty-four hours.

Not everyone you hire will be as energetic as this. And not everyone you hire will be bouncing off the walls. Just make sure the people you hire are energetic and positive.

One more warning: think twice about consultants, especially those who come from outside the Internet. In the brick-

and-mortar world, consultants are teased because they don't do anything—they just talk about doing things. And when they try to jump to the Internet things only get worse. Not only have they not done anything, they haven't done anything *fast.* I've actually had consultants hand me twenty-page, graphics-filled, PowerPoint presentations. They're beautiful but a total waste of everyone's time. I don't have time to wade through that much paper, and anyone who can't get his ideas down in one or two pages has way too much time on his hands and isn't a good match for the Internet.

2. **Hire your friends. Hire your employees' friends.** Even under the best of circumstances, you can't get much information about a potential candidate besides his or her overall energy level and industry knowledge. And as quickly as we sometimes need to hire people, that's not nearly enough. That's why I firmly believe that the best predictor of future success and culture match is past success. At Beyond.com, 80 percent of the executives and directors came on board either because I knew and had worked with them or because one of the executives had. The chief information officer (CIO), for example, used to work at mutual fund giant Franklin-Templeton. And when he joined Beyond.com he brought six of his star performers with him.

Traditional human resources "wisdom" frowns on hiring friends. It smacks too much of nepotism. It might cause conflicts of interest or ruin friendships. But my experience, and that of most Internet CEOs I know, says just the opposite. Friends (and this includes trusted people who've worked with or for you) who were stars at their previous company are likely to be stars with you. Plus, if you're going to be spending eighteen-hour days working with someone, you'll have more fun and be a lot more productive if you've already had a successful working relationship and can skip the getting-to-know-you stage.

Growth in the Internet is explosive, and every CEO I know has more open requisitions (budgeted, approved openings) than he could possibly fill. When Beyond.com bought BuyDirect.com, one of the investors asked me whether we were going to bring over all seventy of BuyDirect's employees or lay some off. I almost laughed. At that time we had over a hundred open reqs, so we integrated BuyDirect's seventy and tried to hire more. Anytime we have the chance to hire someone who's a proven, prescreened performer, we jump.

This hire-your-friends rule applies at every level of the company. Beyond.com's Empowerment Division (aka personnel) even offered a nice financial incentive to employees who referred someone who was hired.

3.   **Interview for "back of the envelope" skills.** Like Microsoft and Amazon.com, we became famous at Beyond.com for asking strange questions during interviews. I've been known to ask candidates to tell me how many stoplights are in the city of San Jose or how many sesame seeds are on a Big Mac bun.

You'd be amazed at the variety of answers I got. When I asked one guy the stoplight question he gave me an answer instantly: 250. When I asked him how he came up with that he shrugged and said he'd guessed. Someone else started asking me all sorts of follow-up questions: Did I want to include stop signs, too? Was I counting only the downtown area or was I including the surrounding area? And on and on. Five minutes later she hadn't given me an answer. Plenty of others just stared at me. They'd prepared answers about where they expected to be in five years or what their strengths and weaknesses are; they weren't expecting questions about stoplights.

None of these people got the point—or the job. I wasn't looking for the exact, right answer. In fact, I couldn't care less what it is. When I ask a question like that, I'm really trying to find out how fast you can think, how well you think things through, and whether you can keep your composure when faced with the unexpected. Instant answers based on nothing are useless, and so are brilliant answers that take too long to reach.

What I look for is what Yahoo!'s CEO, Tim Koogle, calls "similitude," meaning that you don't have all the facts so you have to come up with an educated guess. An example of similitude might look something like this: "Well, there are probably twenty north-south streets in the city and twenty east-west ones. For the sake of discussion, let's say there are four hundred intersections and that one in four of them has a light. So I'm going to say there are a hundred lights." Again, I'm paying attention to the process rather than the answer.

At Beyond.com, I had to make hundreds of decisions every day, from what we should merchandise on a particular page and whether we should do a one- or five-year portal deal, to how many engineers we'll need for the next quarter and whether we should increase or decrease our new employee stock options. Should we, for example, sign a deal with Lycos that will cost us $1 million but will guarantee us 100 million page views? Hard to say. We can probably assume that 2 to 5 percent of them will link to us and that another 2 to 5 percent will buy something. But will they spend enough so we can get our $1 million back? And how many of them will come back and buy again so we can get a return on our investment? We had to make a decision right away. What do you do?

Internet managers are hit with dozens of questions every day that have no easy answers, and so are the people who work for you. If they're going to be able to keep their heads above water at all, your key people have to be able to make decisions that are fast and smart. Winning on one count isn't enough. You have to win on both.

4. **Reduce transaction times.** In the Internet world speed drives everything in every department of every company—even human resources (HR), which is traditionally not known for its speed. At Peoplesoft, though, they addressed this

problem, having new employees enroll for benefits on-line before they show up for their first day of work. This means that employees can start working right away instead of filling out papers. And every month at Beyond.com, everyone in the company would sit down over pizza to discuss important issues. The first time we did this all the pizzas were put on one table and there was such a mob scene that it took twenty-five minutes for everyone to get served. I was furious that we'd wasted so much time. We changed to serving the pizzas from ten tables and the wait became less than four minutes.

These reductions may seem insignificant, but in a high-pressure industry, where every minute counts, there's no room for wasting time. Even a few seconds. By cutting down the pizza waiting time, 350 of us had an extra 21 minutes of productive time added to our day—a total of over 120 hours. An awful lot can be accomplished in 120 hours.

Once you've reduced some transaction times, keep looking for ways to improve. Like many companies, Beyond.com started a weekly newsletter that went out to all employees. But instead of getting a hard copy (which would mean someone spending a lot of time printing, copying, collating, and distributing), we received the newsletter electronically. At first we e-mailed it to everyone, and that seemed like a great solution. But sending HTML files to 350 people at the same time put a real strain on our system—we could literally watch the internal server slow down as the newsletter was being sent. And that affected every single person in the company. So we switched to what the people in the Valley call "Post, don't Publish": we post the newsletter to our internal web page, send everyone the URL instead, and invite them to read on-line.

Making your company and your employees more efficient is only part of the solution. You've got to do the same for yourself. There are, of course, lots of little repetitive tasks you could do less often. If you fill up your tank when it's one-eighth full instead of one-quarter full you'll make fewer trips to the gas station. If you get more cash out of the ATM you'll spend less time standing in line. And you can save yourself a time-consuming trip to the polls on election day by getting an absentee ballot and voting while you're on an airplane.

Consider, also, subscribing to an abstract or clipping service. Why should you spend valuable time reading entire trade magazines just to find the one or two articles that you're interested in when someone else can clip them out for you? And if you're like me, there are dozens of great business books you've got stacked up by the side of your bed that you know in your heart you'll never get to. And why should you? You can subscribe to abstracting services that will provide you with a two-page summary of a book's key points that you can read in a few minutes.

Looked at in isolation, these may seem like trivial little time-savers, but once you start looking for and finding more opportunities to save time, you'll discover that you've freed up enough minutes for you to think up the solution to a non-trivial problem.

5. Have power coffees, not power lunches or break-fasts. A lot of nutritionists are saying that grazing—eating lots of small meals throughout the day—is healthier than eating three big meals. The same can be said about meetings: lots of short coffees (or teas, or bagels, or whatever you like) are far better than a few full-blown breakfasts or dinners. Here's why:

▷ They're a lot less formal. As a result, your body language, hand gestures, and even your vocabulary are going to be far more relaxed and conducive to partnerships.
▷ Because the time is shorter, you'll be more focused and be able to get more work done per minute than you would over breakfast or lunch.
▷ You can have three or four power coffees in the time it would take you to do one breakfast or lunch.

▷ You can politely walk out of a power coffee after fifteen minutes. Just try that in a power meal!

I have power coffees with all kinds of people: CEOs of other Internet companies, venture capitalists, and entrepreneurs. And once a month I had coffee with Bill McKiernan, the chairman and founder of the company. If Beyond.com's stock price was up the day before, he would buy; down, I would.

And finally, one of the best things about power coffees is that no matter how many you have you'll still have plenty of room to take in an entire power breakfast or lunch if you really have to.

⑥□ **Boot up your computer and be on-line in under thirty seconds.** With e-mail an increasingly important part of life—you'll be sending and receiving it from airports, hotels, living rooms, and bedrooms—it's particularly important to reduce the time it takes you to dial into your company server and retrieve your e-mail. On the hardware end, the trick is to buy only machines that have a standby mode, which will enable you to reboot right back into your e-mail program instead of having to start from scratch every time. On the server end, the trick is for your engineers to design for minimal time for user identification, password checking, and connection to your company's Intranet. Before Beyond.com made these changes, it sometimes took three or four minutes to go through the whole process of turning the computer on, dialing in, getting access, calling up and connecting to the e-mail program, and starting to download e-mail. We achieved under thirty seconds. Guaranteed.

At this point you're probably thinking, "You're nuts, Breier. Couldn't you just get a cup of coffee or make a phone call or go to the bathroom while the computer is booting? Are you really so strapped for time that a couple of minutes waiting for your computer to boot up will make a difference in your life?" Absolutely.

I can't tell you how many times I've been on the road and had literally only one or two minutes to check my e-mail between meetings. In fact, on insanely busy (and even normally busy) days, a long start-up cycle is simply a disincentive to log on. If you know it's going to take more time than you have, you might not even bother.

The cost of not being able to check your e-mail can be enormous. Once Beyond.com lost the chance to hire a key manager because I didn't have time to log on. I needed to sign off on hiring a key executive we'd been courting, but because I didn't respond to an urgent e-mail, the rest of the management team—and the candidate himself—assumed that my silence meant no. He took another job.

7. **Set up e-mail power sessions.** E-mail is one of the most powerful tools you have, allowing you to communicate with many people at the same time and helping you resolve issues quickly. But in order to benefit from e-mail's potential, you absolutely need to carve out blocks of time *every day* to do nothing but respond to e-mail, at least the most urgent ones. I receive as many as two hundred e-mails per day, and while some of them are useless, there's always something that needs my immediate attention. So set up half-hour power sessions three or four times a day. (I do it as soon as I get into the office, at lunchtime, at the end of the day, and at night after I put my kids to sleep. And I schedule an extra-long session on Sundays.)

8. **Quit making long-term plans.** One of the first things Jeff Bezos gave me when I arrived at Amazon was a marketing plan that had been prepared by my predecessor. It was impressive, more than fifty pages long with a detailed discussion of the category, our consumers, the marketplace, and a thorough analysis of each of the previous year's marketing tools and the next year's strategies. I was impressed. Jeff hated it; he was showing it to me as an example of "paralysis analysis." "The company is growing 25 percent a month," he said. "It took six weeks to research and write this thing, and during that time the whole business had changed. Nothing in it applied anymore."

In traditional businesses, spending two or three months researching and writing fifty-page strategic, marketing, and financial plans complete with one-, three-, and five-year projections is still the norm. It's a clear, methodical, ready-aim-fire way of doing things. In the Internet age, however, it's ready, fire, aim. Long-term forecasts are pretty much a thing of the past. Things are changing so quickly that it's impossible to accurately forecast any farther out than the next few months or so. As a result, I focus on quarterly, and to some extent annual, plans. (I'll sometimes recommend creating three- or five-year plans but almost always just to satisfy an investor or banker.)

There are relatively few points that your business plan needs to cover: How big is the category? Is it growing or declining and at what rate? What percentage of the market is going on-line? How much market share do you have? How much revenue are you bringing in, what's your gross margin (before sales and marketing, general and administrative, research and development costs), and what's your net margin? Answer these questions for the previous several quarters, the current period, the next quarter, and the long-term (one to two years out). Do *not* spend months or even weeks doing this. You don't need fancy graphics or charts. You probably don't even need a fancy binder. You can put these plans together in three or four days, with nothing sloppy or shoddy about them.

⑦. **Set very specific goals and pull out all the stops to accomplish them.** Back in 1998, when Software.net was just about to go public, we had the opportunity of a lifetime: to work with Microsoft and AOL and to launch Windows 98 on AOL's pop-up screens. These screens have become one of AOL's most coveted pieces of real estate. They hit you with a sales pitch even before you get the "You've got mail" voice, and you can't move on until you click something, whether it's "Tell Me More" or "No, Thanks." Microsoft also wanted us to fulfill their back-office orders for Windows 98 and we knew we couldn't pass up the opportunity to get over 8 million impressions in a few days' time. That kind of volume had the potential to net us tens of thousands of orders.

But the hurdles would have sent many companies cowering in fear. Until then, Beyond.com had been handling only about a thousand orders a day, and we'd have to dramatically upgrade our technical capacity to handle the increased volume. And in case that wasn't enough pressure, Microsoft was screaming for us to create incentives to push the product because they wouldn't allow a price break. We had only sixty employees at the time, and most of the top executives were consumed with the road show and initial public offering (IPO) preparation. Those who were left were completely exhausted trying to make sure we made our quarterly numbers in advance of our IPO.

But we weren't going to let a few obstacles interfere with our goal of establishing ourselves as *the* brand for digital downloading, to become synonymous with our category. And to do that we were going to have to rethink every aspect of what we did and how we did it. We'd have to install a new server, create new customer service pathways, and work with our marketing partners to increase our ability to send them orders without completely crashing our respective systems.

So we put together a team of about twenty people from throughout the company and told them they had just a few weeks to pull it off. Jen, the project manager, kept her tired and frustrated crew moving forward by bringing in breakfasts for the 8 A.M. team meetings. Every single day, multiple people threw their hands up in exasperation and predicted we'd never finish in time. But we did. And we made our quarterly numbers and we successfully went public.

While this story is certainly about speed and commitment, it's also about something that's crucial to making people move quickly. You absolutely must have and set very specific targets. Don't tell your technical crew you want "faster" page-load speeds, tell them you want pages to load in less than four seconds. Don't tell them you want the necessary upgrades done "as fast as possible," tell them you want the site's capacity to be at least ten times the forecasted traffic volume. And specifics aren't just for thriving on the Internet. If you don't like what's happening at your children's school, don't tell school administrators you want "better" school scores, tell them you want a 35 percent improvement in three years. And remember, also, that focus is important, particularly in a constrained engineering environment. Doing a few things right is preferable to finishing late or with lots of software bugs. Designate one person (often the chief operating officer) to do the weekly triage and embrace the few, most important projects.

10. **Don't be afraid to make mistakes.** Once a decision presents itself, don't overanalyze. Make a decision now rather than weighing it for too long. In traditional business, people put off making a decision until they absolutely have to. Tim Harrington, the CEO of Fogdog Sports, spent sixteen years at IBM where he says the decision-making philosophy was: ready, aim, aim, aim, aim, aim. . . . By the time they fired the target had often moved. In the Internet world, on the other hand, it's sometimes closer to ready, fire, aim. In other words it's not as important to get it 100 percent right as it is to get out there and do something fast.

Sparks.com was one of the very first on-line greeting card companies. In a hurry to firmly establish the company, CEO Felicia Lindau launched an advertising campaign before she had a chance to do focus groups and get live feedback. The ad slogan was "Don't settle for the wrong card." It sounded good, but customers didn't like the negative message. They wanted a positive "do" message, not a "don't" one. Sparks.com changed their campaign immediately.

Because being the first mover in your category is so critical, failure in the right cause is excusable, as long as you learn from your failures and act quickly to rectify them. One of the great things about the Internet is that because you get feedback so quickly, you can make changes almost immediately.

ЛЛ▫   **Slow down.** Being a top-notch Internet CEO is similar to being a top-notch speed-chess player: you have to have a bias toward action and you've got to make your moves quickly. But speed isn't everything. You've got to size up the situation, weigh your options, and consider the consequences of each of those options before you do anything. As the pressure to act grows, so does the potential to make stupid decisions. Acting quickly—just for the sake of doing something—is not the answer. Acting fast without acting smart is worthless. Sometimes even harmful.

One of Beyond's competitors, Outpost.com, found this out the hard way. In a hurry to establish a brand name in the category, they put together a series of television commercials designed to etch their name into the public consciousness. You may remember some: gerbils getting shot out of cannons, babies having their heads tattooed, wolves chasing a marching band. Most people found the ads tasteless and offensive and the company received highly critical, scathing criticism in the media.

Some projects simply can't be rushed. As John Pettitt, Beyond.com's chief technical officer (CTO), said, "Having a baby takes nine months. You can't do it in one month with nine women." If Outpost had done some focus groups—something any fresh-faced MBA would have known to do—they might have saved themselves a lot of money and a lot of damage to their reputation.

Reacting to competitors, or rather overreacting to competitors, is another risk of moving fast. When I was working with Jeff Bezos at Amazon I was always amazed at how few stupid things got done despite the incredible pace. But there were a few. One happened when Barnes & Noble put out a press release announcing that it was offering an 88 percent discount on some titles. Jeff became obsessed with beating them, and he ordered us to find titles we could offer for 89 percent off. We scrambled for catalog ideas, redid the site, and shot off hundreds of press releases. Ultimately, though, no one cared—especially not our customers. But by the time we'd figured that out we'd already wasted two days of work, days that would have been far better spent on something more productive.

At Beyond.com, we bought Buydirect, a local competitor, in March 1999. But we were instantly slowed down by the new management demands and engineering integration. One conventional wisdom says that it takes at least six months to integrate an acquisition. That proved true, but it was an "Internet time" six months and slowed Beyond.com at a critical growth period.

Internet companies are building the airplane while they're flying. Categories and companies are changing rapidly. In 1997 Beyond.com had sixty employees. By the end of 1999 we had four hundred. Back in 1997 we were mostly packers and shippers and order-takers for cellophane-wrapped boxes of bytes. By 1999 over half of our business was digitally transacted—and I mean fully transacted: browsing, ordering, delivery, payment—on-line and within a few minutes. At the same time, Beyond.com had raised $250 million in two public rounds and a convertible debt offering.

It's hard to imagine this kind of growth. But there's no time to think about it. Internet companies are in a twenty-four-hour-a-day race for mind share. The eventual Internet winners need to act fast and act smart. And whether or not you run an Internet company, if you're doing business in the Internet age, you will, too.

12. **Eliminate mediocrity**. As important as hiring fast and hiring smart is eliminating poor performers quickly.

Most managers know whether an employee is a "keeper" within thirty days. It is to both of your benefits to act quickly if the person is not producing the results at the pace your company needs. This can be difficult and counterintuitive, because you usually have many more open slots than you have bodies. But the speed of the Internet magnifies the positive or negative impact of each employee.

For more tips on acting fast—and to share tips of your own—visit *www.10secondmanager.com/fast.*

CH@PTER **2**

E-MAIL
MORNING, NOON,
AND NIGHT

Talk in between

So how does a guy who's too impatient to read *The One Minute Manager* get time to write an entire book? Well, a lot of it was written on airplane runways when the weather was bad, and at home, late at night and early in the morning, when I probably should have been sleeping. But I also wrote a lot while at traffic stoplights and while I was waiting for pickup basketball games to start. Whenever I had a few seconds I'd jot down my thoughts and e-mail them off to my cowriter. If e-mail didn't exist, this book wouldn't either.

In the Internet world, CEOs and just about everyone else uses technology to turbocharge productivity. We all have our laptops, our pagers, our Palm Pilots, and our cell phones. (Jeff Bezos taught me the value of having a "hotline," a cell phone at your hip the number of which you give to only the thirty key people in your life: your spouse, your executive assistant, your board, your executive team, and your key suppliers.)

41

But e-mail is by far the most valuable technology of all. Sure, sometimes it's a little overwhelming (sometimes a lot) to start off the day with 250 e-mails waiting. But there's a lot more upside than down. Without e-mail I simply couldn't manage the number of decisions I have to make every day. I'd barely see my family and I probably wouldn't be able to fit in my sanity-saving basketball games. And I certainly couldn't get work done in strange, formerly dead-time places like airport waiting lounges, New York taxis, and during jet-lagged hours on faraway continents.

I came from the packaged-goods world, where I once made an impression as a lightning-fast, mountain mover because it took me only six months to incorporate a *Star Trek* movie promotion on a Kraft marshmallow package. If I worked at that speed now, I would have run a company called Behind.com.

E-mail is the oxygen of Beyond.com and of the Internet as a whole. It's how we talk to each other and to our customers. It's how they tell us how we can serve them better or how we've fouled up. It's how we sandpaper the rough edges off deals and how we can reach out from under the worst, most intense production crunches. I once figured that over 50 percent of my daily conversation is by e-mail. It's one reason I'm able to do so much in so little time and makes it possible for me to aspire to do even more.

Picking up a phone might seem like a faster, more direct way of connecting with people, but it isn't. Have you tried to get anyone on the phone lately? It's almost impossible to navigate the endless layers of voice mail. If you do manage to leave a message, there's no telling when or if it'll be retrieved. Sometimes that's even done by secretaries who transcribe the messages—sometimes accurately, sometimes not. E-mail eliminates that risk and gets your message, just the way you want to say it, directly to the person who's supposed to get it.

E-mail also streamlines intercompany communication and flattens the corporate structure. It's a way of having a bunch of conversations simultaneously. An entire department, for example, can get important news straight from the horse's mouth the same time the manager does. This allows everyone to mobilize quickly and focus on the real problem without wasting time in one of those long meetings where the manager doles out information one point at a time—and puts his own spin on things (which may or may not be the right spin).

Seventy-five percent of the 250 to 300 e-mails I got at Beyond.com every day were internal. I could deal with most of them with a one-line response like "Yes" or "No" or "Reschedule this for 1 P.M. tomorrow." That meant that I could sometimes answer ten questions or resolve ten issues in less than a minute. It's not that I didn't want to talk to people; it's just that there's nothing more to say. If all those issues had to be resolved in person or on the phone, I wouldn't have time to do anything else.

Most of my e-mail was fairly low priority: automatic site statistics, Internet newsletters, and unsolicited business solicitations. But there were always some golden opportunities lurking: someone waiting on me for key action, a journalist looking to mention us in an important article or survey, a new idea to build the business, a big partnership proposal, personal greetings from friends, or office flame mail that would burn and grow ever brighter unless I stepped in to extinguish it.

One of the most interesting uses for e-mail, though, is for therapy, to give your employees the chance to let off steam and vent a little without jeopardizing their careers or doing anyone serious damage—kind of like when your mother told you to go in the basement and pound nails instead of hitting your sister.

Most of these therapeutic e-mails are exchanges between middle- and lower-level people who are going ballistic because they've been ordered to do more than they think is reasonable, and to get it done faster than they think is possible. Some of them question their managers' parentage. Or IQ. Or blood alcohol level. In most companies something like that would be considered insubordination. But I've got a special collection of them and I consider them to be incredibly important management tools.

While working one day, I was showing one of these to a friend. It had been forwarded to me by a programmer's manager, without the employee's knowledge. To spare the employee embarrassment, suffice it to say that the message was a concise paragraph along the lines of, "If those f------ a------- think I'm gonna give up another f------ weekend for some f----- up idea about how to . . ."

My friend was shocked. "Does that person still have a job here?" he asked.

"Of course," I replied. "He was right. We were asking him to do something really unreasonable. He'd been working long hours for three weeks and was exhausted."

"Oh, so you backed off the request?" my friend responded.

"Not at all," I explained. "Everyone around here works long hours and everyone gets asked to do unreasonable things. That's why you let this happen. It lets them blow off a little steam and it lets me know that that person basically needs someone to talk to."

I didn't keep these messages because I wanted to hunt down and fire their authors. Some people send flaming screeds whenever you ask them to do anything; that's just the way they are. With other people, though, the smallest shift in tone is meaningful, and I would get up and run over to see what was up. And when it comes to the everyday pressures of our business, I knew that if I asked for something that's truly crazy I would hear all about it via e-mail, even from folks who'd probably never muster the courage to tell me to my face.

Used correctly, e-mail is a ruthlessly efficient way to get

issues handled in your company. But there are risks. You can't have employees using your system to harass people, solicit sex, or commit any of the other virtual deadly sins. That's obvious. More important, though, if it's overused, e-mail becomes like tribbels (from *Star Trek*) or kudzu (an invasive vine)—multiplying so quickly and so powerfully that they choke out all other life forms.

It wasn't all that long ago that you could still meet high-tech CEOs who proudly walked around telling everyone, "To tell you the truth I don't use e-mail." Today, making a comment like that in the Silicon Valley might get you arrested.

The best companies use e-mail from top to bottom, and the only Internet CEOs who are going to make it have incorporated e-mail into their toolbox along with their pager and their heartless cost-cutting chief financial officer (CFO). One of the biggest clues to whether I can and want to do business with someone at an Internet company is whether he or she uses e-mail the way I do: in short, intense bursts at least three or four times a day. It separates the savvy managers from the "don't get its."

Amazingly, too many CEOs are still holdouts. They don't have e-mail addresses or they have their assistant handle it for them. These folks don't get the power of the Internet and they'll be quickly run over by those who do.

Felicia Lindau, CEO of Sparks.com, actually puts everyone in her company through a course on e-mail management. If you work for Sparks.com you might not need to read the rest of this chapter (although you'll probably learn something anyway). For the rest of you, here are some tips for using e-mail that are guaranteed to improve your information flow and productivity. And don't keep these ideas to yourself. The more people in your company who know about—and start implementing—them, the more productive everyone will be.

∄▫   **Put the topic and desired action in the Subject line.**
Imagine that you're in a hotel on the other side of the country;
you call in to check your voice mail and find fifty messages. Or
imagine that you walked into your office after a long lunch and
your secretary has covered your desk with dozens of those little,
pink message slips. How can you possibly tell which ones need
your attention right away, which you can get someone else to
take care of, and which you can simply ignore? It's the same
with e-mail. If all fifty messages in your in-box are titled
"Thought you'd want to see this" or "A few questions for you,"
there's no way you'll be able to figure out which ones need to
be handled first. And that could cost you more valuable time.

Some time ago, Beyond.com was having a problem with
AOL: they weren't generating enough traffic for us and, as a
result, our cost per customer was edging up. We needed to
resolve the problem immediately, so I sent AOL's CEO, Bob
Pittman, an e-mail with the subject "Needs urgent attention
to preserve our relationship." He got back to me within minutes. I can just about guarantee that if I'd written "Partnership
update" or "Per-customer costs" I might not have heard from
him as quickly.

Being clear on what you want is just as important with
intracompany e-mail. If an HR executive had a great interview
with a top-notch person and wanted to hire him to fill a critical position, he would e-mail me the person's résumé and put
"Needs your approval on new department hire" in the Subject
line. Before I even open the e-mail I know exactly what he
wants (to hire someone) and what he wants me to do (to
approve it). I trusted the Beyond.com HR people, so I would
take a quick look through the résumé and sign off on it in one
minute. If I had received the very same e-mail but with a
generic "Check this out" in the Subject line, it would take a lot
longer to resolve.

In addition to helping me prioritize, good Subject lines
make it a lot easier to organize important e-mails and to find

them again quickly if I need to refer back to them. I don't file a lot of paper anymore—seems like I sometimes go days without seeing any. But I do file a lot of e-mail. One final note: don't go overboard and make your Subject lines too long. Keep them to seven words or less.

2.   **Be concise.** I'm a great believer in the Three-Paragraph Rule: if it takes you more than three paragraphs to make your point, you're taking too long. One reason for this is that it violates one of the Internet's "golden rules": don't make people use the scroll bar for important information. The more important reason is that rambling on and on shows a certain lack of respect for other people's time (and for mine). If you don't have anything to say, let me get back to work. I don't know *anyone* in the Internet world who wouldn't like to be able to get through his e-mail faster.

Beyond.com once had a major site outage and thousands of our customers were inconvenienced. We were committed to keeping our customers happy, so we planned to send out a letter to them, over my signature, apologizing for the delays and telling them how much we'd improved the site. I asked the customer service people to draft the letter and they came up with an incredibly detailed, technical memo that read like *War and Peace.* Here's a *small* sample:

> While evaluating our site in preparation for the holiday shopping rush, we discovered the need for some fine-tuning. Over the past two weeks, we have made major improvements to our technology, stabilized the site, and even reconfigured our database. We can now process over twice as many simultaneous orders, and we have even reduced the ordering process time by one third. We take great pride in these accomplishments, but that pride is tempered by the fact that the implementation of these improvements was not transparent to our valued customers.

Still awake? Here's the same paragraph from what actually went out:

> You may have experienced difficulties on our site last week while we upgraded for expected holiday traffic. We apologize profusely. The good news is that our upgrade was successful and that the new Beyond.com site is now running better than ever.

That's it. Short and to the point. No one really wants or needs to know the intricate technical details of why the site went down. All they care about is that they were inconvenienced. And all we really need to say is we're sorry and we hope they'll come back.

And since we're talking about keeping things brief, try not to send attachments unless it's absolutely necessary. Sometimes a Beyond.com employee would send me attachments with elaborate Excel spreadsheets analyzing daily customer counts in fifteen-minute increments. That didn't help me at all. I'm not going to go through a spreadsheet like that. What I really need is a paragraph summary: tell me, concisely, what we learned and what are the implications. Are customer counts going up over time? Are there certain peak periods? What's the average wait time? Don't send the data when all I need is the news!

3. Don't spend too much time worrying about the rules. In the early days of e-mail no one cared about grammar or punctuation or even spelling. Things have come along since then but it's still a very casual means of communication. If e-mail had a dress code it would be Internet casual, just like the actual dress code in most Internet companies: a few steps above cutoffs and a T-shirt but less formal than a suit. When writing e-mail you should consider your audience. You'll use a different tone when inviting a coworker to lunch than you would when sending a formal response to a buyout offer. Either way, you don't have to be so formal that you sound like British royalty, but at the same time you don't want to appear incompetent or stupid by misspelling simple words or putting together incomprehensible sentences.

Once you put something in writing you'll never know what will happen to it or who will see it. So choose your words carefully and, if you're e-mailing something particularly important, take an extra few seconds to use your e-mail program's spell checker and proofread it.

4. **Don't contribute to e-clutter.** Do you remember the story of the Chinese peasant who saved his emperor's life? The emperor was so grateful that he offered to give the man anything he wanted as a reward. The peasant made a seemingly modest request: take a chessboard and put one grain of rice on the first square, two on the second, four on the third, doubling again and again with each successive square. At first the emperor thought he'd gotten off easy, but after a while it became clear that he was in serious trouble. The installment for square 32 was over 2 billion grains. And there wasn't enough rice in all of China to make it all the way to square 64.

A charming story, but what does this have to do with e-mail? More than you might think. E-mail has a nasty way of multiplying, and it doesn't take long to get completely out of control. So here are a few things you can do to keep e-clutter from taking over your life.

▷ **Don't copy people who don't really need it.** Because it's so easy to add names to a cc: list, and because it doesn't take any more time to send fifty copies than it does to send one, people sometimes get careless and end up sending e-mail to many, many people who don't really need to get it. Of ten people who receive a single piece of e-mail, three of them will respond to the sender, five will delete it, and two will forward it on to ten more people —the original ten doubled. If that continues, well, you can see where this is going. . . . Being more judicious in deciding who *really* needs to be copied certainly saves wear and tear on your server, but more important, it will end up saving your employees a lot of time responding to, forwarding, and deleting e-mails they shouldn't have received in the first place.

Also, encourage employees to avoid using cc:s as a political statement. Almost every day I would get copied on an e-mail correspondence that had absolutely nothing to do with me. In some cases, the only reason I'd be copied is because people think that by running and telling the teacher just like they did in kindergarten they'll get the upper hand in the argument. It rarely worked and often made me wonder more about the tattler than the tale.

▷ **Reply to sender, not all.** Just about every office has e-mail distribution lists. They're wonderful for spreading the word to the whole company about things like blood or toy drives, open enrollment for the health plan, or who's the new employee of the month. Lists are also great for quickly getting information out to smaller groups of people—the engineering group, marketing team, key managers—who might be affected by a particular issue.

Most of these e-mail announcements are for information only and don't require any action on your part. Sometimes they do. But before you click on Reply to All, think about whether everyone in the company needs to read your personal note to Jenny congratulating her on the birth of her new baby. Or whether the entire executive group needs to know you've got a medical appointment and won't be able to make lunch this afternoon.

If everyone else did the same, you'd all be bombarded with e-mails that you really don't care about and that would take a lot of your time to delete.

▷ **Add value when forwarding.** One of the most valuable business lessons I learned while I was at Kraft was that good managers add value to everything that goes through their hands. If you clipped an article out of the *Wall Street Journal* that you thought would interest someone you know, you'd probably mark the relevant parts of the article with a highlighter or put a Post-it on it with a note about why you're sending the article.

Why not do the same with a piece of e-mail? Before forwarding a message you received on to someone else, ask yourself why you're sending it, what you want the person receiving it to do, and when you want them to have it done. Put your comments, views, recommendations, or suggestions right at the top.

And finally, if you subscribe to the joke-of-the-day or the recipe-of-the-week list or are addicted to downloading JPEG (large graphic files), great. But keep it to yourself and don't forward these things on to everyone in the company. On the flipside, get yourself off any lists you don't want to be on. (Most have an unsubscribe link at the bottom. If they don't, take twenty seconds to send the company an e-mail asking to be taken off. It's worth it in the long run.) And be careful when checking out Internet sites. Most of them will ask you whether you want to be on their mailing list and will assume "Yes" unless you specifically click "No." Whatever you do, find out whether your e-mail program has a filter function and learn how to use it.

5. **Check your e-mail every two or three hours. More often if you can.** As an Internet manager, you've got a lot of decisions to make, and there are a lot of people waiting for you to make them. The more often you check your e-mail, the shorter your company's decision-making cycle time and the more efficiently your whole company can operate. Every day between 7 A.M. and 9 P.M, I'd check my e-mail at least five or six times—and that's an absolute minimum for survival. You simply can't possibly operate at Internet speed if you don't do this.

Checking your mail from home in the evening is important. You never know when little emergencies or interesting opportunities are going to crop up. At 7 P.M. one night I got an e-mail from Jerry Yang at Yahoo! inviting me to a meeting at ten the next morning with Secretary of State Madeline Albright. I'd never have been able to make it if I hadn't checked my e-mail until the morning of the meeting.

Don't check your e-mail just before you go to bed, though. You probably won't be able to respond to anything major until the morning, and whatever it is you read, no matter how trivial, you'll end up thinking about it all night. The Internet owns your life while you're awake; don't let it get control of your sleep, too.

🕕 **Take action.** One of the first things an efficiency expert in a traditional office will tell you is that you need to take action on every single piece of paper that crosses your desk: respond to it, delegate it to someone else, delete it, or hold off on making a decision. With e-mail it's basically the same. As we discussed in Chapter 1, set aside three or four half-hour blocks of time where you do nothing but go through your e-mail. As you retrieve each one, quickly decide which of the following options best applies:

> ▷ **Delete.** That's pretty obvious, isn't it?
> ▷ **Divert.** File it away or give it to your assistant to file. Steve Jurvetson, a partner at Draper Fisher Jurvetson, puts all the e-mails from people he doesn't know

into a separate file to be dealt with over the weekend. Diversion is also for things that you don't really need to look at but would be good to have around for reference just in case.

▷ **Delegate.** Put the monkey on someone else's back. But make sure the person who assumes ownership of the task knows precisely what the expectations and time limits are. And make sure everyone knows who's in charge of that topic.

▷ **Do.** When you send an e-mail, how soon do you expect to get an answer back? Because e-mail has shortened communication times, people have begun to have unrealistic expectations for response times. If at all possible set a target of responding to as many e-mails as you can within four hours. Some, of course, you'll get to quicker. But the longer you wait, the lower the chance you'll respond at all. If I e-mail Michael Dell or Tim Koogle at Yahoo!, I know I'll have an answer back in less than twelve hours. I once sent something to Tim late on a Friday afternoon, but he was away and didn't get back to me until Monday. I didn't really care because what I sent wasn't urgent, but Tim was apologetic. The point is that waiting too long to answer defeats the whole purpose of having sent the e-mail in the first place.

Each department should set its own response-time goals. But keep in mind that most people who e-mail an e-commerce company assume that the second they click "Send," their e-mail has been received and is being worked on. They expect an answer within twelve hours—especially from customer service people. Not getting one back within seventy-two hours is considered just plain rude, and a week's delay is a sure sign of incompetence.

▷ **Deliberately—but not accidentally—delay.** This may be the trickiest one of all. When you get a magazine in the mail, you probably don't sit down and read it right away. You put it in the pile of things you'll get to within a few days. Plenty of e-mails are like that, too. If you decide not to deal with a piece of e-mail within your four-hour time limit, give yourself a specific deadline by which you will make a decision about what to do. Do *not* just let things sit in your in-box imagining that they'll somehow take care of themselves. They won't. They'll multiply just like the grains of rice on the emperor's chessboard.

You might want to set up a two-tiered system for delaying. E-mail I get from people I don't know or whose names I don't recognize, for example, I put in a folder to clean up over the weekend, when things are somewhat less hectic. As a general rule, though, if the messages in your in-box are more than forty-eight hours old, you're moving too slowly and you're going to get bogged down.

7. **After the third e-mail on the same subject, walk 'n' talk.** Bill Joy, cofounder of Sun Microsystems, is fond of saying, "In most conversations you think I'm saying what you want to hear and I think you're hearing what I want to say." Basically, conversation is dysfunctional. It's a lot worse with e-mail. Beyond.com's Gordon Jones would cite research that more than two-thirds of all communication is nonverbal. It's all in the body language—the gesturing hand, the raised eyebrow, the quivering lip, the sweating brow, the dilating pupils, and all the other things that convey huge amounts of information that words alone couldn't possibly do. So while e-mail is great for yes and no answers, there are plenty of times when words just aren't enough, no matter how articulate you are. Those ridiculous emoticons— :) and :(and ;-) and 8-) — may help pick up the slack a little, but they're rarely enough.

As a result, e-mail conversations sometimes go on well

past the point of increasing marginal returns. Here's a summary of one correspondence I was cc:d on at Beyond.com.

One exec suggested to another that we include some people who aren't managers in the managers' meeting. The second agreed, sort of, but wanted to know where the line would be drawn. The first suggested a list of ten people from the finance department because they'd been involved in making some very big decisions. The second agreed, sort of, but wanted to take a few people off the list and add some others. What was clear to me (but obviously not to them) was that the conversation was going absolutely nowhere and could have continued to go nowhere for days.

In his first couple of weeks as Egghead's CEO, George Orbin banned e-mail from the workplace, saying that no one was talking to each other anymore. Personally, I think George was overreacting. E-mail can be an incredible communication tool. (Apparently George came around; he lifted the ban after only a few months.) But he does have a point: sometimes you just have to talk to each other.

That's why at Beyond.com we had the Three Strikes Rule. If each person has sent three e-mails and you're still haggling over the issue, it's time to get out of your chair, walk down the hall, and figure things out face-to-face.

If you institute this rule at your company, your employees will probably be able to take care of most of these problems by themselves. Still, there may be times when you'll have to get involved. Every once in a while I'd be copied on a series of e-mails. I'd sit back and watch for a while because a lot of times they're actually violently agreeing but just talking past each other. If it goes on longer than three exchanges, I'd step in and suggest that everyone involved in the discussion get together in person to work things out.

8.   **Establish ownership.** In any organization there are departments that sometimes seem to be working at odds with each other. Operations wants to build something that's fast and reliable. Marketing wants it to look pretty, and the software engineers want to develop something interesting. Most of the time all these goals can be accomplished. But sometimes it seems as if they're mutually exclusive. And that's when the blaming starts.

Often, what begins as a simple disagreement quickly escalates into an all-out flame war. The exchanges get more and more hostile, other people get dragged in, and, ultimately, the company gets less and less productive.

Fortunately there is a cure. I've found that a large percentage of employee conflicts come about because no one is quite sure who's responsible for a particular thing, and they end up lashing out at each other in frustration. By assigning ownership—clearly defining who has responsibility for a particular project and the authority to make decisions—you can often step into the middle of a flame war, remind everyone who's in charge, and tell them to direct their questions and all further correspondence to that person instead of to each other. It's like capping an oil fire with a small blast of your own.

9.   **Get a separate account for your personal stuff.** You're probably so busy that you don't have time to deal with your personal stuff at the office, but sometimes there's no choice. Still, if you find yourself taking care of personal business using your company e-mail, you should strongly consider stopping.

First, whenever you send anything—even something personal—via your company e-mail system, it's as though you're putting it on company letterhead. The company owns it and they're responsible for it—they even own the copyright to it. If you say something illegal, the company could be liable, and if you happen to get sued, the plaintiff could demand it in discovery.

Second, there's a copy of every single e-mail you send or receive on your company's server. Every once in a while you have to fire someone. It's not something you like to do and you should try to keep it out of the trade press. Once, at Beyond.com, we had to let one of our executives go. He was barely out the door when the news was all over town. Apparently someone had forwarded a private e-mail to CNet—a strict violation of company policy. Leaking internal information that affects the company's reputation in the investor community is a fireable offense. Anyway, it didn't take us long to go through the outgoing e-mail on the server and track down the culprit.

Another reason for getting a separate personal e-mail account is that you never know when you're going to find yourself out of a job, and out of the company e-mail account that went with it. Again, the company owns your e-mail and they'd be well within their rights to read anything that happens to come in after you've left. So get yourself a solid, external e-mail address that will be yours no matter where you're working.

10. Praise in public, criticize in private, or, when not to send e-mail at all. Because e-mail is so easy to use and so casual, too many people use the Send button before they've thought things all the way through.

A star mid-level department head at Beyond.com sent me an e-mail with his plan on how to reorganize the whole company from top to bottom. He even included suggestions on which departments should be closed and which VP positions eliminated. Unfortunately he cc:d every VP in the company, including those he thought should be fired. Within twenty minutes, five VPs had crashed into my office demanding that this manager be fired immediately.

I told the guy's supervisor to handle this right away and to

have him immediately apologize face-to-face to everyone concerned or walk out the door. He chose, instead, to send yet
another e-mail, which just got him into even more trouble. I
finally brought the guy into my office—something I should
have done the minute I got the first e-mail—and we talked.

He recognized that it would have been completely inap-
propriate to have sent out the very same memo on company
letterhead or to have presented his ideas face-to-face to anyone but me. The sad thing is that his proposal was interesting
(theoretically, anyway) and I would have been glad to discuss
it with him in private. But he took the wrong approach. By
sending his ideas to the executive team and making his criti-
cisms public, he'd seriously set back his relationship with a lot
of key people in the company.

The bottom line is that you should *never* use e-mail when
you're angry and *never* write anything that you wouldn't send
on company letterhead or that you wouldn't want everyone in
the company to know about. Because e-mail can be forwarded
and can spread quickly, you have to assume that anything you
send is public—or soon will be.

Remember also that the written word can be awfully lim-
iting. If you write something you really don't mean—or that
someone takes the wrong way—it can be very hard to undo.
Something that's intended as a joke may strike the person who
reads it as distinctly unfunny. So if you've got a suggestion for
how to change the world or you're angry about something or
you've got something private to discuss, set up a time to talk
in person.

Although I've spent most of this chapter discussing the
ways to manage your e-mail internally, don't make the mistake of underestimating how important e-mail is to managing
relationships with people outside your company—suppliers,
marketing partners, advertisers, and, most important, your
customers. It's with e-mail that you'll be able to let your cus-

tomers know about site improvements, new products, and special offers. Using e-mail gives you the opportunity to connect almost instantly with your customers and encourage them to tell you what you're doing right and what you're doing wrong.

For more tips on e-mail—and to share tips of your own—visit *www.10secondmanager.com/email.*

MAKE FEEDBACK
YOUR FRIEND

*J*ust after taking over as CEO of Software.net (which became Beyond.com a few months later), I sent out the following e-mail to a number of recent customers:

Dear "K":

I would like to introduce myself, say a brief thanks, and ask for your advice. I recently joined Software.net (http://www.software.net) as president and chief executive officer (formerly, I was VP of marketing at Amazon.com). I'm very happy to be here.

So let me begin by saying "thanks" for shopping with us. I know firsthand that having lots of happy customers is the key to our success. My personal goal is for each of you to be an ecstatic customer.

I would like your advice on how to make Software.net the absolute best place to purchase software. In recent weeks, we've made some improvements. We made our website faster and easier to use. We added a quick-buy feature for returning customers, and, most important, we made it easier to download software. I am sure that you have other ideas on how we can "wow" you. Please visit our improved site and tell me what you like, what you don't, and share with me any new ideas you have.

Again, thanks and I look forward to achieving your highest satisfaction.

Mark Breier, CEO

It didn't take long for "K" to respond:

You are full of shit, sir.

You never answered my e-mail and I can't reach anyone at your business to help me! I will be speaking to our state's attorney.

K

I absolutely hate what happened to "K," but I love his letter. And I love showing it to people who think that customer service and feedback aren't important. Unfortunately, though, that's not an attitude shared by many businesses today. They don't focus enough on customer service and they don't spend enough time trying to figure out what customers want. Worst of all, they don't ask for feedback. Instead, they let themselves get defensive, bureaucratic, and lazy. And in the process they leave the door open for fast-moving, customer-focused outfits to eat their lunch.

Word of mouth is the single most important customer acquisition tool companies have. It's better than television, radio, or any other type of advertising or promotion. When we asked new customers why they came to our site, the number-one answer—by far—was "because a friend told me about it." The same was true at Amazon, and I'll guarantee you that it's the same at AOL or eToys or any other e-commerce site.

And I'd bet that the opposite is true, too. If we could ask people who had bought their software from one of Beyond's on-line competitors why they hadn't bought from us, one of the top reasons would be "because a friend told me not to." From the sound of it, "K" probably sent his e-mail a few months before I asked for his feedback. And while we were ignoring him he was telling his friends about his miserable experience or posting angry comments about us on chat boards. I can't say exactly how much of an impact treating "K" badly had on our business, but I'm sure we lost a few potential customers.

When I was responsible for marketing Kraft marshmallows, soliciting customer feedback was an extremely time-consuming and expensive process. We'd get a monthly recap of phone calls and letters and it would take literally six months to figure out whether a promotion worked, and even then our only clues were changes in warehouse volumes, which were measured by the ton—hardly the most subtle way to gauge anything, especially marshmallows. To get customer feedback, we'd have to hire market research firms to send armies of clipboard-toting interviewers out to malls or grocery stores, or hire dozens of telemarketers to survey thousands of people, many of whom don't even buy marshmallows. Tabulating the results would take months. And making any changes would take even more months, assuming we were able to change anything.

In the Internet world, though, getting feedback is fast and easy and a lot cheaper than the clipboard method. In minutes we can gather statistics on the exact number of customers who buy from us, what they buy, how much they spend, and whether they come back. As a result, we could tell almost instantly how well a particular promotion is working. You should be able to automatically gather and analyze this kind of data in-house. There are also several third-party companies—Accrue and E.piphany are the best known—that can set you up.

More important, you can solicit customer feedback and complaints and get an up-to-the-minute look at exactly how you're doing from the people you're trying to please. If Beyond.com made a site improvement, the site department would put together a short questionnaire that we asked customers to fill out at some point during their visit. If we were introducing a new product, our new product department would put the questionnaire together. The questionnaires consisted mostly of questions customers answered on a 1 to 7 scale (How happy are you with our new look?) and a very few narrative questions (What about the look do you like or dislike?). But before any survey would go out to the site we would test it in-house by having ten employees go through it and let the appropriate person know if the questions were clear and the process of answering smooth and painless.

Once the data started to come in, the speed of doing business on the Internet would allow Beyond.com to respond to make any necessary changes virtually overnight.

As an Internet CEO (or any other kind of CEO, for that matter), there's no excuse for not fundamentally understanding your customers, for not knowing what they want, and for not acting promptly on the information you receive. At Beyond.com we used video terminals around the office to display our "customer happiness index," which is based on sales, complaints, returns, and a few other measures. We asked customers to give us a 1 to 7 rating (where 1 means extremely dissatisfied and 7 means extremely satisfied) in three areas: how happy they were with their Beyond.com experience; would they buy from us again; and would they recommend us to others. We averaged the results and would always know how we were doing in the eyes of our customers as well as compared to our established goals. Figuring all this stuff out isn't rocket science. All you have to do is ask for some feedback.

And when you're thinking about feedback, don't forget about your employees. They've got a lot of important things to say, too. Not asking for—or ignoring—their comments, complaints, ideas, and suggestions is almost as big a mistake as not paying attention to your customers. The following tips will give you some surefire ways to get your customers and your employees talking.

GETTING FEEDBACK FROM YOUR EMPLOYEES

1. **Set up an anonymous, electronic question box.** In a perfect world, everyone in your company would feel comfortable enough with each other that they could ask someone a question about something that's bothering them or give a little constructive criticism without fear of retaliation. But it's not a perfect world. People do worry that complaining will get them in trouble. As a result, instead of raising important issues with their supervisors or anyone else above them in the chain of command, they'll complain to their friends or simply stew while their resentment and anger build.

The simplest solution to this problem is the anonymous suggestion box. A lot of companies have them; Beyond.com made theirs electronic to save time collecting pieces of paper and organizing them. Employees sent their suggestions or comments or questions to a special e-mail box that automatically stripped the sender's identifying information.

The issues that came up were generally personal and

ranged from the minor—"We need a bigger coffeepot because we're running out in the morning," or "Can we bring a dog to the office?"—to the major—"What are you going to do about my 'underwater options'?" (If an employee was given stock options to buy at twenty and the stock is currently at ten, his options are considered under water, since there'd be no sense in redeeming them.) Sometimes they had to do with spending issues, such as whether the company should give Snapple to people instead of Coke, which costs half as much. And sometimes they had to do with relationships between employees and their supervisors or coworkers. But big or small, each question is important to someone, and that makes it important to the company.

What almost all the question box comments had in common was that they mostly had to do with why certain things were being done a particular way. Getting an answer—even if it's not a particularly satisfying one—gave employees a greater sense of control over their work environment. They knew that no question they asked would ever be out-of-bounds, and that their comments and concerns would be taken seriously. That made them feel better about the company and made them happier to work there. I've worked for people who absolutely refused to have an anonymous suggestion box at work. They couldn't imagine that people might not feel comfortable bringing up an issue face-to-face, or publicly, in front of three hundred other people. Obviously, I disagree.

At Beyond.com we sent out a reminder about the question box a few days before our monthly all-hands meeting and we would usually get ten to twelve questions, which we made part of the agenda. Every question was read to the whole group and was resolved in some way or other.

2. **Have regular meetings.** In Chapter 4, we'll talk about meetings and how to structure them for maximum efficiency. But here, suffice it to say that I have a lot of them. Once a week

I would have a three- or four-hour meeting with the members of Beyond.com's executive team. We would have a standing agenda, but before we started, people were free to add topics they'd like to discuss that day and those topics got discussed during the meeting.

Every two weeks I had breakfast with fifteen or twenty people who had their birthdays around then. I made sure everyone knew everyone else and what they do, which would help keep me (and everyone else) from getting too out of touch. I would talk about the company mission and handle any questions or concerns. We would have an open dialogue about what was working at the company and what was not. This is a really great idea that I got from John Chambers, who does the same thing at Cisco. The logic is that grouping people by birthday as opposed to job category or team is a great way to get people together who work in different kinds of positions in all kinds of different departments who might have no other reason or opportunity to meet each other.

And every month Beyond.com got together for a pizza lunch. This was where we'd introduce new employees and new products and recognize major accomplishments. Most important, it's the place where we'd publicly answer the questions from the anonymous question box as well as answer any others that people would raise. While I wanted to try to respond to every issue, I didn't read questions that were mean-spirited or deliberately designed to publicly hurt someone. And if a question complained about a specific person by name, I'd always change it to something more generic, such as "one vice president."

On Thursdays at Fogdog Sports, employees gather for an informal (and company-paid) lunch where they can get updates on what's happening with the business and answers to any of their questions.

Each of these meetings has a different purpose and a different agenda. But what they all have in common is that they remind employees that we—from the lowest-level employee to the CEO—were in it together. They also gave our employees regular opportunities to speak their minds. As a result, they became absolutely essential tools for obtaining employee feedback. Employees knew that, as with the suggestion box, they could say anything they wanted with no need to fear negative consequences.

3.   **Do 360-degree reviews.** In most companies, performance reviews are one-way, top-down phenomena: the CEO reviews the vice presidents, vice presidents review the managers, and the managers review the front-line employees. At Beyond.com—and a number of other Internet companies (it's pretty common in the Valley)—we did what we called "360-degree reviews." In this type of review, each person receives feedback from above, below, and from his or her peers. As with customer feedback, most of the questions are quantitative and use a 1 to 7 scale to rate such qualities as integrity, bias toward action, and management skills. We would also ask the reviewer to briefly discuss such nonqualitative issues as what the person being reviewed does to help the reviewer, what hurts, and what the person isn't doing that he or she should be doing. All these reviews were done anonymously, on-line, and were compiled and tabulated by an outside service.

We also would review ourselves. Each person then received an individual score and an indication of how that score compared to the average score for other employees on the same level. Interestingly, the self-reviews were almost always the harshest of all.

Many people find this system very threatening when they first hear about it. But after the first review, everyone loves it. One reason is that it gives people a chance to learn a lot about themselves, their effectiveness, how they're perceived, what their strengths and weaknesses are, and how they rate on such important skills as follow-through, leadership, and communications. In a traditional review, an employee finds out only how he manages "up" (how he gets along with supervisors). In a 360-degree review, employees get a chance to see how they manage up, down (how effective they are in managing the people they supervise), and across (how they get along with their peers). This is a very important concept in any industry, but it's even more important in an Internet company. Because we work so closely together for such long periods of time, peer relations are especially important. At Kraft, I might have conversed with my Operations counterpart once a month. At Beyond, it was five or six times a day.

Best of all, the 360-degree review gives employees a lot of control over their own development and growth within the company. After the reviews are in, the most important part of the process begins. Employees sit down with their bosses, discuss what they learned from the 360-degree review, and propose their own action plan to improve whatever needs improving. When I met with people who reported directly to me, I would ask them to tell me three of the areas they're strongest in, three "opportunity" areas, and the area in which their self-rating was farthest from the average comment they heard from others. I would add my comments and make a few suggestions, but most of what came out of the review was generated by the employee.

GETTING FEEDBACK FROM YOUR CUSTOMERS

If there is one single benefit of e-commerce, it is "convenience." It is far more important than price (as proven in Amazon.com and Beyond.com studies and in Internet industry research). And the key to finding out what convenience means to your customers is asking them for feedback: what's working, what's not working, and what can we do better.

1. **Ask for it.** You can divide your site's visitors into two groups: those who buy and those who don't. You need feedback from both.

As a general rule, e-commerce sites get twenty to fifty times more "lookers" (visitors) than "bookers" (buyers), and it's important to get to know who they are, what causes them to visit, and, of course, what makes them buy. When you're soliciting feedback make sure you get enough—you can't just ask five or six people and get much of a feel for the issues that concern them. On the other hand, you don't need answers from every single person who comes to your site. As a compromise measure, you might want to have some kind of a short survey that pops up on every fiftieth or one hundredth visitor's screen. (Be careful with pop-ups, though. Felicia Lindau, head of Sparks.com, says that while they generate lots of great feedback, they also anger up to a third of the people who get them.)

You're looking for answers to questions such as: What brought you to the site? Are you just browsing or did you want to buy something specific? Did you find what you were looking for? Did you buy something? If not, why? What can we do better? Every visitor to your site is not only a potential customer but, even if they don't buy something, a wonderful source of advice on how to improve your site. Be sure, though, to make your surveys short and to the point. The more time people spend filling out your survey, the less time they'll spend buying.

There are two basic ways to encourage customers to answer your questions. You can tell them that their answers will help all future shoppers (customers like to feel they're influencing others and this approach is usually quite successful). Or, you can "spiff" them, which means offer them a reward—usually a discount certificate or a chance to win something. Customers should also have the option of opting out (not participating) completely.

If you're spending a lot of time analyzing your data, you're doing something wrong. Your surveys should be set up with multiple-choice answers that can be automatically tabulated and averaged. The only thing that might slow you down is reading the occasional narrative answers you'll get. As I've said before, you should be able to manage this operation in-house. (At Beyond.com and most other Internet companies it was done by the market research department.) If you can't or don't want to, there are several companies, such as Bizrate.com, that will do it for you for a fee.

While getting feedback from general visitors is important, it's even more important to get it from people who've actually bought something. That's why about two weeks after every sale Beyond.com automatically sent out an e-mail letter to customers asking them about their purchase experience. Did they easily find what they were looking for? Was the process easy to use? Would having a voice guide them through have made it easier or would it have been annoying? Was their order delivered on time?

Too many companies make the mistake of assuming that making a sale is the same as making a customer happy. The truth is that people who buy are frequently *not* happy at all. Overall, the quality of customers' purchasing experiences will determine whether they become evangelists (people who tell all their friends how wonderful your site and everything about it is) or terrorists (people who do exactly the opposite, bad-mouthing you to as many people as possible). We'll talk more about this below.

Another frequently overlooked source of very valuable feedback is customers who bought from you but who haven't been back to your site for three to six months. Quite simply, we want to know why not, and Beyond.com sent an e-mail to every one of them asking exactly that. Are they buying from our competitors? Are they buying from stores? Did we do something to offend them? Interestingly, the most common reason people gave for not having come back to the site was that they simply hadn't bought any more software products since then.

Knowing the answers to these and other questions can not only improve your site, it can also help you more accurately determine how much you should pay on a per-person basis for customers referred to you from other sites.

And finally, make sure customers can offer their feedback at any time—not just in response to one of your surveys. Have "Contact us" or "Give us your feedback" options on order forms and sprinkled throughout the site.

2. **Set up a heavy-user group.** No matter how much you solicit customer feedback and how nice you are in asking for it, there comes a time when customers will be a little annoyed at all the e-mail they're getting from you. (Beyond.com tried to let customers know about site improvements, new products, and new features and all those mailings can get overwhelming—especially considering all the other e-mail they're getting from other .com companies.) Long before you ever get to that point, come up with a small but reliable group of people (forty to fifty) you can turn to for regular, brutally honest feedback on your site. You're going to ask more detailed questions about products, services, and technical aspects of your business than you typically ask in a regular customer survey. Make it worth their while by giving them discounts on products or, perhaps, first dibs on hot, new items.

The people in your heavy-user group can be friends, family, tech people who work at other companies, or customers with whom you've developed a truly good relationship. Software enthusiasts and power users take pride in being asked for their opinions and are usually very willing to participate. I also was asked my opinion on a number of occasions by customers who really wanted to join us in some kind of official consulting capacity. If, after exploring all these options, you're having trouble getting enough people together, you can probably recruit some by sending a direct e-mail invitation to some of your best customers.

Not everyone has to compensate their heavy-user groups. At Charles Schwab, investors with assets over a certain amount are invited to join Schwab's invitation-only Mutual Interest Council. Once each quarter, Council "members" get a short e-mail survey to fill out, giving feedback on a variety of investment-related areas. There's no compensation, just a nice-looking invitation to join, the good feeling of being asked to join, and the feeling that by participating you'll be helping yourself (mutual interest, right?) as well as Schwab. And you'd be right: by participating, members undoubtedly give Schwab up-to-the-minute information on how best to serve—and keep—their customers.

Microsoft uses heavy-user groups a lot, particularly to get feedback on beta versions of new software products. These testers are usually techies who love having the chance to play with a program that hasn't hit the street yet. (They're the same people who'll spend two weeks living in a tent outside a movie theater so they can get tickets to the first show of *Star Wars: Episode 1*.)

3.   **Do it yourself.** There are many outside research firms that would be glad to collect customer feedback for you. Since you won't want to give out your customer lists (there's too much information in there that your competitors would kill to get their hands on), the research company will probably send out 10,000 or 100,000 e-mails to random e-mail addresses, many of which don't even belong to your customers, so you'll be lucky to hear back from 1 percent of them. You could end up with some great feedback, but there's also the risk that if the people who get your e-mail think it's spam, you'll have alienated them even before they ever have a chance to buy something from you.

Getting a private firm to do your research will probably cost you about $50 per respondent, meaning that two hundred answers will set you back $10,000. The big question is why you'd want to pay anything at all. You already have the names and e-mail addresses and buying patterns of your customers, why not use them?

4. **Keep the customer in the loop.** All that feedback you gather is absolutely worthless if you do nothing with it. Beyond.com added voice prompts at the beginning and end of the download process, for example, because a number of customers had complained that they couldn't tell when the software they'd just bought was through downloading. A lot of eToys customers used to complain that their children recognized the logo on the boxes and tore into them before they could be wrapped. Reluctantly, but wisely, eToys took their logo off their shipping boxes. Fogdog Sports received so many requests for hockey equipment that they "built" a hockey store six months earlier than they had planned to. And Sparks.com removed a series of drop-down menus from one part of their site because customers said they wanted to see all the choices on the screen without having to pull anything down.

Customers who respond to your surveys or who offer unsolicited feedback want to know that they're not just sending things off into some black hole. So if and when you make changes based on customer recommendations, let them know— not just the ones who responded to the surveys, but everyone.

One way to do this is to put the word out in your regular newsletter. Something like, "Last month we asked you how to change our site. Well, thanks to your suggestions, we've made the following changes . . ." The Beyond.com newsletter is put together by the customer communications team within the marketing group and usually includes notifications of improvements, features, and sales. Before putting out each edition of the newsletter, the customer communications folks collect information from any and all departments that have news or information to share with customers.

5. **Make your customers part of your team.** Not all the feedback you want from your customers should be about you, especially if you're in some kind of e-tail business. As part of the automated postpurchase survey Beyond.com asked customers to give their opinions on the products they bought (Are they satisfied? Did they work as advertised?) and to rate them on a one-star to five-star scale. Beyond.com compiled all the data and posted an average consumer-rated score next to every product on the site.

Amazon.com and Beyond.com go one step farther, encouraging visitors to actually post their own reviews right on each product's page. It's one of Amazon's most popular features. And Biztravel.com has a special forum where travelers can post their comments—nasty or nice—about airlines, hotels, restaurants, etc. Beyond.com considered expanding the forum section so customers would be able to post questions or problems they were having with specific hardware or software and get help and advice from other customers.

Including your customers' reviews and rankings on your site has several significant benefits. First, it makes customers feel that their vote counts and that they're a valued part of the operation, which of course they are. This, in turn, makes them more loyal. Second, using a customer-driven rating system removes an element of suspicion many customers have that you're giving some products high marks for the wrong reasons: maybe it's because you get a kickback on sales or because your margin on that product is particularly high. Using customers' ratings gives them an opportunity to learn how the products they're considering perform for real people in real-life situations instead of in some lab somewhere. And they're right.

Simply put, asking for—and posting—customer feedback makes your site more useful and more attractive to your customers. In a sense, it's also an indicator of whether you really have the Internet mind-set. Traditional retail business may ask customers for overall feedback, but they'll almost never ask their customers to rate individual items, because displaying negative comments about a product anywhere near it (or anywhere at all, for that matter) could potentially drive away business. That's a concern you generally don't have in the e-commerce world. Since you handle many, many more products than traditional stores, you don't care *what* customers buy. You just want to help them find the product that best fits their needs.

6. **Use the speed of the Internet.** Yet another wonderful advantage of the Internet is that it allows you to solicit and incorporate customer feedback without even asking for it. Sound crazy? Let me give you an example.

In mid-December one year, Beyond.com wanted to introduce a new product for people who'd waited until the very last minute to buy holiday gifts. It was essentially a virtual package: the recipient would click on a button and a beautifully wrapped "present" would open up on their screen, followed by instructions on how to download their software present. The problem was that our marketing department had come up with two different versions and we didn't know which one would be the most successful. Would customers be more likely to order one of these gifts if we pitched it as a "great way to do last-minute shopping," or as a "cheaper, more environmentally friendly way to send holiday gifts"?

We sent out five thousand of each version and the convenience version generated twice as many sales as the environmentally friendly one. We also got a number of e-mails from customers telling us about a few things that had confused them. We made some changes and sent out the "last-minute" promotion to the remaining hundreds of thousands of people on our list. From start to finish, the whole thing took forty-eight hours. In the traditional world, it would have taken months.

AOL did this kind of research to determine whether it would be better to offer prospective customers a $50 discount or fifty free hours. If you've opened your mail lately, you know which one won. Consumer catalog companies (L.L. Bean, Lands' End, etc.) do this absolutely brilliantly in the real world. Some of them have applied their direct marketing savvy to their Internet business and are among the top e-commerce sites as a result.

7. **Have your managers get their hands dirty.** I was once head of marketing for Cinnabon, a company that, not surprisingly, makes cinnamon buns. The restaurant business is agonizingly, painfully slow. But I learned an important lesson. I think of it as "goo training."

Once a year, all of Cinnabon's senior managers would go to the central kitchens and learn how to make gooey cinnamon buns and frost them. There's nothing like getting covered in sticky icing up to your elbows to give a smug, suit-wearing young executive an appreciation for what front-line store managers do every day.

At Beyond.com we didn't have any goo, but each of the senior managers spent a few hours a month reading and responding to customer e-mail, handling problems and requests, soothing bruised egos, and paying close attention to what the customers were saying. At Fogdog, CEO Tim Harrington goes one step farther. He automatically gets a copy of _every single_ customer-generated e-mail that comes into the company. He doesn't read all of them all the way through, but even skimming them gives him a real feel for his customers' wants and needs.

The range of issues that comes up is amazing: program compatibility problems, confusing directions, inability to navigate our system, downloading disasters, products that never arrived in the mail, things taking too long to happen, and more. Hearing all these things and having to respond to them gives a management team regular reminders that without happy customers we don't have a business. With that in mind, managers can make customer-focused decisions, as opposed to decisions that might make the marketing department's or the engineering department's or the designers' lives easier.

8.   **Respond ASAP.** Besides customer counts, conversion rates, and average purchase amounts, one of the most important statistics Beyond.com tracked was the percentage of customer e-mails we responded to within twenty-four hours. Obviously, the higher the percentage the happier our customers would be. We shot for 95 percent and I think that's a pretty high standard. But Meg Whitman, CEO of eBay, insists they answer 95 percent of their customer e-mail within *twelve* hours.

Divide your incoming customer e-mail into several categories: those claiming "you're the best company in the world" can wait a day or two. They're from evangelists who will tell all their friends about you. It's the e-mail from the venom-dripping terrorists that must be handled immediately. If you catch the problem soon enough, you have a pretty good chance of turning a terrorist into an evangelist.

The way to do this is to go out of your way to provide a prompt, courteous resolution to your customer's problem. Amazon is absolutely amazing about this. Besides a sincere apology, inconvenienced customers might get a reduced rate on shipping costs, a coupon for a discount on their next book, or even the book they ordered at no charge.

Every once in a while, though, you'll get a customer who makes repeated complaints when there really isn't anything wrong. He just likes getting the discounts and rebates from you. If this happens, you might want to take a note from Nordstrom, the king of customer service, and gently tell these malcontents that you've made every reasonable attempt to satisfy them, and if that isn't enough, you may not be the best fit for their needs.

Most of the time, though, it doesn't take all that much to satisfy an angry customer. In fact, sometimes they don't even need to have their problem solved; they just want to know that someone is listening. So if you don't have a specific answer or solution to the customer's problem, be honest. Tell them you don't and let them know when you will. Here's a good example:

In the heat of one Christmas-buying frenzy, Beyond.com got an angry e-mail from "C," who hadn't received the software he'd ordered for his family. Trying to avert a potentially nasty episode, one of the customer service people jumped on the case immediately.

Dear "C,"

Thank you for considering Beyond.com for your software needs!

I would like to apologize for the difficulty with your order.

All of the items but Ultimate World War II Game were shipped out yesterday via UPS 2 day air. You should receive them on Monday by the latest. The Ultimate World War II Game is still on back order and we do not have an ETA as to when it will be available. I apologize for all of the problems that occurred with your order.

If you have any further questions, comments, or concerns please let us know.

Regards,
James M.
Customer Service
Beyond.com

Just a few hours later "C" replied.

Dear Mr. M.,

Thank you, thank you! Your e-mail has made my night and taken a load off my mind. It is great news to know that I will have the gifts for my family in time for Christmas!

Again please accept my sincerest thanks to you and any other members of your staff who may have assisted in expediting my order for me. Seasons greetings to you all and I look forward to doing more business with your company in the near future.

Sincerely,

"C"

One Now Happy Customer

One less terrorist; one more evangelist.

9. Tie employee compensation to customer satisfaction. Every single employee at Cisco Systems is evaluated based on the happiness of the company's customers, and their bonuses are structured accordingly. You can bet that their employees are soliciting customer feedback—and making changes—every chance they get. Of course, it's a little easier for them to get feedback than it is for us. They have only a thousand or so customers (although they're pretty enormous customers) while Amazon and Beyond have several million.

As I said in Chapter 1, the Internet world is moving so quickly, it's almost impossible to gather all the data that's needed to make a decision. The problem is that if you don't act—with or without everything you need—someone else will. You may not get it right the first time, but because the Internet and e-mail allow you the incredible opportunity to gather your data on the fly, you can get it right the second time. So instead of ready, fire, aim, you actually end up with ready, fire, aim, reload, aim, fire again.

Without customer feedback you can't survive in the Internet world. The minute your customers realize they can't get what they want from you, they'll move on to someone who can give it to them. Entire industries have been created simply as a result of some clever entrepreneur satisfying a particular group's unmet needs. We'll talk more about that in the branding chapter. Constantly soliciting and responding to the things your customers tell you will at least keep you a step ahead of your competitors and keep newcomers from cannibalizing your market share.

For more tips on making feedback your friend—and to share your own tips—visit *www.10secondmanager.com/feedback.*

CH@PTER 4

THE SECRETS OF EFFECTIVE MEETINGS

t's 8:30 on a Tuesday evening and I'm sitting at a conference table at Amazon.com with the rest of the executive team. I'm tired, I'm hungry, I'm bored, and I really want to go home and see my family. But this meeting is going to last another hour. Jeff is up at the white board talking about something I lost interest in twenty minutes ago. He's on topic number nine. Out of twenty. Did I say an hour? We'll be here at least two.

During the time I was at Amazon the same thing happened every Tuesday night: a 5:30 P.M. meeting that would usually go until 9:30. Jeff had the idea that if he had meetings when people were tired they'd be more productive because they wouldn't argue about anything unless it was really necessary. He also felt that he didn't need to feed us during these evening meetings ("Other late-night workers aren't being fed so why should you?" was his argument). Someone once ordered in some Chinese food, but she nearly got her head bitten off, so no one tried that again.

Jeff Bezos is a guy who is usually right. But I think his ideas about evening staff meetings were wrong. Tired people are far less productive. They're cranky, emotional, less likely to cooperate with each other, and more likely to make quick, poorly thought-out, and less-creative decisions just to end the suffering.

It's no small wonder that meetings are the bane of many employees' work lives. Too much time, too much discussion with too little action, too little respect, too much finger-pointing, too many late arrivers, and too many people who talk too much or make meandering speeches that have nothing to do with what's being discussed. If there's a hell, it's probably an infinite number of two-hour meetings, one right after the other.

Unfortunately, though, meetings are a necessary evil. You can't run your company without them. Every day at Beyond.com I would have three or four single-issue meetings on topics as diverse as site scaling (increasing the amount of traffic we could handle), new product development, and advertising. And I was not alone—just about every manager in the company was juggling a similar number of meetings.

Since all these meetings generally involve more than one person, it's pretty obvious that they take up a lot of time for a lot of people. But that's not all. They take up a lot of company dollars, too. This point was first driven home to me when I worked at Dreyer's Grand Ice Cream. At the beginning of every meeting Rick Cronk, the president of the company, would look at his watch and say, "Looks like an expensive meeting. Let's get started so we can get this thing over quickly." To give us an incentive, Rick would tape twenty-dollar bills to a wall in the meeting room. "Finish your presentation early, take a bill," he'd say.

I once did some quick calculating on the back of an envelope while waiting for a plane and figured out just how right Rick Cronk was. Let's say you gather ten mid-level managers together for a typical two-hour meeting of wandering discussion and little closure or follow-up. On salary alone, that meeting is costing you $500. With benefits you're up to $800. Add in a reasonable allocation for company overhead (the CFO is going to be so proud of me for mentioning that) and a little extra to cover visiting executives' time and one simple meeting is setting you back $1,000 to $2,000.

If you really want to get exact, you're going to have to run your own cost-of-meeting (COM) calculations. But that's not a productive use of your time. The point is that meetings are expensive. And if you take into account the number of meetings that are happening somewhere in your company _every_ day, well, you can see where I'm going with this. Averaging just one meeting a day will cost you $5,000 to $10,000 a week. Take that out to a year and your COM can easily run up to half a million dollars.

Because things in the Internet world are moving so fast, Internet companies simply can't afford to have unproductive meetings. They can't afford the time or the money. Following the tips below will help you reduce the number of meetings you have, make them shorter, and keep them as efficient and productive as possible.

$1.$ **Sell your meeting.** If we go on the basic assumption that your employees' top priority while they're at work is to actually work, it's clear that at the very least, meetings are competition. So apply some basic free-market principles to your meetings: if you want people to come to them, you'll have to convince them that it's a worthwhile and productive way to spend their time. Don't assume meetings are a given, that people will drop whatever they're doing at a moment's notice and herd into a conference room like a bunch of sheep.

So, when announcing your meeting, stay away from non-specific phrasing, such as "There will be a meeting at three this afternoon to discuss a new home page design and a few other issues." Instead, try something more specific and goal-oriented, like "Today at three we will choose the home page design from the two remaining options, set the go-live date, and determine who has responsibility for the site's feedback function."

The difference between the two options is that the second presents very clear goals and outlines specifically how those goals will be accomplished. It also tells people that if they have a stake in the issues to be discussed and want their vote to be counted, the only place to be at three o'clock is at your meeting. Anyone who can't make it has options: not to be counted or sell *you* on the idea that the meeting should be rescheduled.

2. **Let people "opt in" or "opt out."** Now and then you'll have a meeting that everyone has to attend. But mandatory meetings should be rare. Most of the time you should leave the door open for people to opt out if they have a conflict or if the meeting really has nothing to do with them. The "in or out" option should be available to all employees, not just managers or other big shots.

Because of the insane pace in the Internet world, about a third of the people who got invited to my birthday breakfast meetings opted out. At Kraft or any of the other traditional companies I've worked for, almost no one would have had the guts to turn down a meeting with the CEO, assuming, of course, anyone actually ever saw him. At Beyond.com, it was different. Everyone knew that it was perfectly fine to tell me that they couldn't make the meeting because they were on a tight deadline. We would reschedule for another time.

Opting in or out shouldn't be an all-or-nothing deal. There's nothing worse than having an overloaded, crazed work schedule and having to sit through a meeting while people hash over stuff that doesn't concern you in the least. At Beyond.com, if a meeting started at 10 A.M. and your topic was covered at 10:15, you took off. No one thought you were being rude. We respected people who knew where they were most needed and who knew how to prioritize their time.

And don't consider your invitee list set in stone. You may occasionally have to instantly recruit someone who wasn't originally part of a particular meeting. Sometimes in the middle of a meeting a topic will come up that needs a quick answer from someone who's not there—usually a technical person. Rather than delay acting on this issue or shelving it altogether, pick up the phone and call or go down the hall and bring the person you need back to the meeting.

3. **Plan your meetings in advance.** You wouldn't have people come to your house for dinner without first planning the meal, right? Well, it's the same with meetings, particularly standing or regularly scheduled ones. A few days before the meeting, put together an agenda of the points you want to talk about and e-mail it to everyone who'll be attending. Ask them to contribute any additional points they'd like to discuss. As the meeting host, you'll have to decide which topics you'll be able to get to and which are off point. Five to seven topics per meeting hour is the maximum. Then circulate the new agenda to everyone.

This serves three important purposes. First, it gives you, as the meeting leader, an outline to use in preparing for the meeting. The more prepared you are, the more focused and efficient your meeting will be. Second, everyone attending will know exactly what's on the agenda and will be able to prepare their questions, explanations, or answers. This also gives them a far greater stake in the meeting since they're aware that they're not only expected to actively and intelligently participate, but that they're ready to do so. And third, people who should be at the meeting but who can't attend will know the issues you'll be addressing and will be able to follow up with one of the attendees about the issues that concern them.

Sometimes, of course, you won't have enough time to get

everyone's input on the agenda. If that happens, you'll need two pieces of high-tech, twenty-first-century technology to bail you out: a white board and a big, fat felt pen. The minute the meeting starts, post the agenda on the white board and ask people if there's anything else anyone would like to add. You'll have to assess on the fly which of the new items deserve to be discussed and which are off point. (If you're not the one running the meeting, insist that whoever is follows this rule.)

This all may seem painfully obvious, but you'd be surprised at how unobvious it is to some managers. I've been at more than my fair share of meetings that had more items on the agenda than could possibly be covered in a week. And I've been at meetings where there wasn't any specific agenda at all. Besides making your meetings shorter and making them run smoother, having a clearly focused agenda is a sign of respect for everyone else.

4. **Start 'em—and end 'em—on time.** In the Internet tornado it's often hard to start anything on time, but at Beyond.com we figured out a way to keep our meetings pretty much on track: anyone who walks in late gets charged $5 unless he or she has a truly great excuse. "Sorry, I was negotiating a new multimillion-dollar government contract" is a pretty good one. So is "I had to spend some quality time with my cat because she was mad at me for being out of town on a business trip all last week and was tearing up my house." The excuse doesn't even have to be true, but if it isn't, it has to make us laugh. When the excuses don't fly, money changes hands and gets tossed into the company party fund. No one is exempt; I paid $20 in 1999.

Ending meetings on time is just as important. You can't have a meeting that starts at 9 A.M. and goes until it's over. Again, the overall issue here is respect. People are taking time out of their day and away from their work to attend your meeting, and it's rude—and potentially costly—not to stick to your schedule. The results can range from childish retaliation (she was late to my meeting so I'm going to be late for hers) to simply having people not show up at your meetings at all. Once this starts happening, resentment grows, relationships get strained, and people can't work together. In a fast-moving, intense organization that's poison.

5.   **Keep things moving.** Like any exercise, it's important to warm up before getting to the real meat of your meeting. So start with four or five short, relatively easy-to-handle topics. The idea is to get the conversation going and build some momentum before tackling the more substantive issues.

Work through your topics quickly and smoothly. Most decisions can be delegated to the people who own the under-lying area (more on that below). Keep your discussions to a maximum of fifteen minutes per topic, unless, of course, you're meeting with a small group of people and focusing on a single issue. If it's going longer than that, the issue should be taken up in a separate meeting to be attended by the people it most concerns. The rest of the group doesn't need to stay for a more protracted discussion.

As each agenda point is covered, check it off on your white board and write down who owns it and if any action is required. Then ask the group whether they agree. What you've written has to accurately capture what happened or you have to correct it right there. Seems simple enough, but you'd be amazed how many people leave meetings unclear on what was discussed or what anyone's supposed to be doing to resolve the issues that were brought up. Getting the group's consensus on each item will completely avoid the typical post-meeting curse of "I know you think you understand what you think I said but what you heard is not what I meant." In the current business environment no one has the time for this kind of miscommunication.

It's bad enough to have one meeting; if you have to have the same one again because no one knows what happened the first time, you're in big trouble.

6.   Ownership—not action—is the issue. Sometimes agenda items can be resolved by taking a vote (How many think we should get a bigger coffeemaker?). Sometimes they're resolved by finding out what other companies in the Valley do and implementing the same rules (at Excite@Home, for example, employees can have Coke on the house but have to contribute a dollar if they take a Snapple). In every case the final responsibility—"ownership"—for following through is assigned to one specific person.

Unfortunately, though, in fast-growing companies, or any other kind for that matter, there are always too many areas no one seems to own, or if there is an owner, not enough people know who he or she is. With minor issues (who will order the bigger coffeemaker), not having an owner can be a small unpleasantness. On the bigger issues, though, the impact can be enormous.

At Beyond.com, we found a whole slew of very important areas with no apparent owner. And the first one was our website itself! Now, you'd think that in an Internet company one of the first things to be decided would be who's responsible for the website. But maybe because it's so easy no one thought to nail it down. Is it the marketing group? After all, they're the ones selling stuff. Or is it the editorial team? They write all the copy and content. Or maybe it's the design group? They make it look the way it does. Oh, how about the engineering group? They write the code that runs the whole thing.

The same question came up about who's in charge of site scaling (the never-ending job of increasing the traffic our servers can handle at one time). Engineering (software code)? Operations (the hardware folks)? Infrastructure Team (system architecture)? At Beyond.com we decided it's the chief information officer, since he's the one who's responsible for information, systems, and technology. (In fact, we eventually merged all engineering and operations under our CIO, a common new organizational design for Internet companies.) He had to make sure we could handle twenty times more traffic than whatever our forecast was at any given moment. And who's responsible for the overall happiness of employees? Sounds like a personnel thing, right? Nope, each manager was responsible for the happiness of the people who reported to him or her. And we made it clear that each individual was responsible for letting his or her manager know if things weren't going well.

Also, tracking your company's financials is another critical area of ownership. I advise entrepreneurs to integrate a standard ERP package early in the development process. (ERP, or enterprise resource planning software, combines financial, human resources, inventory management, and other backend administrative tasks into one system.) Trying to integrate an ERP system with a custom accounting or inventory management system that you built can bring your company to a screeching halt. Instead of focusing on enhancing your site's capabilities for growth, you will be devoting precious resources to integrating two dissimilar systems. Form your processes and systems around the ERP system. It will not conform to yours.

Making sure that every issue has an "owner" is an essential part of being an effective Internet manager. So as you go through each item on your agenda, make sure the first issue you deal with is "Who owns this?" If a particular issue has an owner (and that's the case most of the time), he or she is the one who handles it. If an issue is homeless, spend a minute or two figuring out who it should be, or simply appoint someone. Getting the ownership issue out of the way early will help your meetings—and possibly your entire company—run more smoothly. Instead of wasting a lot of time on endless discussions you'll be able to turn a particular issue over to one person who will then coordinate what to do with it.

At Beyond.com, most of the owners were VPs of different areas who had the staff and the budget to do what needed to be done. Any questions that came up about database architecture, for example, went straight to the chief information officer. If any discussion was needed, he would take it up with the VP of engineering. Lots of other people—marketing, customer service, and, well, me—would be just thrilled to offer up opinions on what needs to be changed to make things more efficient. But we'd be wasting everyone's time. The CIO owns it. Marketing, customer service, and I could better spend our time elsewhere.

There are, however, plenty of cases where I would assign ownership to someone who's not a VP. In late 1999 for example, the Beyond.com website was down for several hours and a whole bunch of customers were inconvenienced. We wanted to send them an apology and I asked the e-mail manager to head up the project.

Once an issue has been handed to someone, all further questions and comments go to that person alone. He or she then has the authority to do whatever is necessary to get the job done, including getting other people to help. In the case of the e-mail manager, he was able to ask engineering to run a list of the customers who'd had trouble. He also had the final call on whether we'd give the inconvenienced customers a gift certificate with our apology and, if so, how big it would be.

And once the owner has made a decision, the issue can't be brought up at another meeting for a while. Now, this does *not* mean that no one is allowed to express an opinion on anything that he doesn't own. Not at all. If you've got a comment on an area you're not directly involved in, you can send the owner an e-mail or set up a time to talk privately. Outside opinions are welcome, just not in the middle of a meeting.

7.   **Keep it short.** Remember the idea of having lots of power coffees instead of a few power breakfasts and lunches? Well, from my experience—and the experience of a lot of other high-tech executives—Internet companies have a lot more, but a lot shorter, meetings than physical world companies.

In the months prior to launching a new product, for example, the Beyond.com core team would get together from 9 to 9:30 in the morning at least two or three times a week. There's no question that we would get a lot more accomplished in three half-hour meetings than we would have in one ninety-minute meeting. The quick meetings were focused tightly on the issues that needed the most attention, and they provided a quick energy jolt before getting to the rest of the day.

Unfortunately, not every meeting can be handled in just half an hour. But the longer they go on, the less productive they tend to be. You can probably pull off an hourlong meeting without any big problems. But if you're going to go more than two, you'd better have the entire thing very well orchestrated or you're going to start losing people in a hurry.

8.   **Commit, don't omit.** It's not possible, of course, to resolve every single issue that comes up in every single meeting. But don't just cross these unresolved items off your list and forget about them. In cases like these, it is far more important to commit to making a decision than to omit the topic altogether. In other words, you must do something with every item on your agenda—even if that something is nothing. Let me give you an example.

The Beyond.com executive team once got together to discuss a wonderful new feature we'd been talking about developing. This feature, which we simply called The Feature, would enable Beyond.com to make useful recommendations on what software a customer needed. It was a great idea we really wanted to work on, but it would have taken four engineers and quality assurance technicians at least a few weeks to put it together. At the time of that meeting we were already using our engineers to capacity on other projects. You can only fight so many battles at one time, and it was clear that redirecting our engineers, even for something as great as The Feature, would have had a negative impact on the whole company. So we decided to put off making a decision for two months. By consciously delaying moving ahead on The Feature, we enabled ourselves to continue moving ahead on all other fronts.

Every Internet company has 101 projects that are all competing for top billing. Since The Feature was first discussed, it came up—and was delayed—at least five more times. Beyond.com will get to it one of these days. And when they do they'll devote full resources to it. So, pick your fights and pick a time when you can win them.

9. Follow up immediately. Even though the meeting leader is writing each agenda item and its disposition on the white board and getting consensus before moving on, there's still one more very important step: postmeeting follow-up. Within a few hours after the meeting ends, the leader should e-mail everyone who attended a brief, specific summary laying out each issue covered in the meeting, who's handling it, what additional steps (if any) that person or anyone else needs to take, and by when. Here's an excerpt from an e-mail that I sent out once after a weekly executive team meeting:

> *To recap today's marketing meeting: Jim will contact agencies by Monday and present options via e-mail by Tuesday. Mark will interview and decide on an internal ad project team leader by Wednesday. Thursday morning, the team will convene to pick an agency and by Friday, Mark, Jim, and the team leader will finalize target campaign dates.*

10. Make your meetings fun. Earlier, I talked about how John Doerr, venture capitalist to the gods, is constantly moving around in meetings, pacing, fidgeting. Sometimes, though,

Doerr falls asleep in meetings; it's the only time he can rest. But no one—even John Doerr—could fall asleep at a Beyond.com meeting. We usually had too much fun. This doesn't mean we were not taking care of business—*au contraire.* It's just that we figured out that all work and no play makes a dull meeting; people are far more receptive to meetings if they're engaging and entertaining. Here are some things we did at Beyond.com to spice up our meetings.

> ▷ **Invite parody and rebellion.** I would rarely run our company-wide quarterly meetings at Beyond.com. A week or so before the meeting, we randomly selected one of our directors to be the leader. He or she was told to start the meeting any way they wanted—with a skit, a video, a song—anything, as long as it lampooned some executives or at least a key project or company issue. They always rose to the occasion. One woman, who had a secret life as a stand-up comic, had us rolling on the floor, and someone else ran an entire meeting as Martin Short's Ed Grimley character from "Saturday Night Live," complete with slicked-back hair and pants hiked up to his chest.

> ▷ **Share embarrassing moments.** Every new employee introduced at Beyond.com's biweekly company gatherings was invited—well, more like urged or prodded—to share their life's most embarrassing moment. You heard the most remarkable things from people. It's a proven way to instantly welcome people into the family. It not only makes meetings fun but encourages closer relationships and teamwork by giving everyone something to talk about. You just can't walk by someone who you know locked himself out of his house in his underwear without striking up a conversation.

> ▷ **Formalize the fun.** Every Friday afternoon around 4:30 Beyond.com had the Splash. Technically, it was a meeting, but it was really 10 percent business and

90 percent relaxation. We would recognize a particular accomplishment or milestone, but mostly we just hung out, drank a few beers, and unwound after the week. These Splashes often featured jump-rope contests, bubble-gum-blowing competitions, human pyramid challenges, all of which get people from different divisions to interact with each other, which creates even more opportunities to build personal relationships and foster teamwork.

Meetings are a necessary evil. You've got to have them if you're going to run your company or your department efficiently. But just because every other company you've ever worked for had to have meetings doesn't mean you do, too. So before you schedule one make sure it's really important. Could the issue be decided just as quickly with a phone call or by poking your head into someone's office and asking a few questions? And if you decide that the meeting is important, get in, get out, and get on with your day. Like your decisions—and just about everything else in the Internet world—make your meetings fast and make them smart.

For more tips on improving your meetings—and to share your own tips—visit *www.10secondmanager.com/meetings.*

BRAND MATTERS, ESPECIALLY ON THE NET

(Or, never stand too close to a naked CEO)

I am standing in a broom closet practically naked. It's cold and dark in here and I'm suffering the classic cold sweat. I really should have done more sit-ups. Will what I'm about to do destroy my career?

This is not a dream, not a variation on the "I find myself arriving at my final exam naked and I haven't studied" nightmare we all had in college. The broom closet is quite real. It's adjacent to a small greenroom in the West Coast studios of CNBC's "Squawk Box," an A.M. business talk show that runs on cable television. I've been here half a dozen times before to be interviewed about our strategy, our financial performance, the competition—all the things Wall Street can't seem to get enough of. But this time is different. This time I'm about to become the first CEO of a public company—hey, probably the first guest ever—to do a CNBC interview wearing nothing but my glasses, my wedding ring, and a pair of funky blue boxers that say, "Exposing the power of digital downloading."

I'm standing here, shivering in this broom closet, because there is no changing room at this studio. Typically, interview guests arrive in the clothes they're going to wear on camera. But Lise, the PR director, had a brainstorm: Beyond.com was running an ad campaign featuring an actor we affectionately call Naked Man. The gist of the ad was that by using the Internet, you can order software from us at any hour of the day or night, naked or clothed; and if your order is downloaded digitally direct to your computer you not only don't have to go to a store, you don't have to answer the door for a FedEx or UPS guy. The ads were funny and the campaign was wildly successful, in part because of the great job the actor did to give Naked Man a beguiling, happy-in-his-skin confidence. Right at this moment I'd really like to know how he did it.

The PR idea was simple: let's play off the Naked Man campaign and get you on TV half-dressed to talk about digital downloading.

There's a knock at the door and I come out of the broom closet. Lise is standing there with a photographer who starts clicking. A sound guy from CNBC approaches me with a small, clip-on microphone. Houston, we have a problem. I narrow my eyes and think as loudly as I can, "Nipples are not an option." Having apparently read my mind, he dashes off and returns a few moments later with a roll of white adhesive tape. "No way," I say. "It'll look like I'm wearing a heart monitor." He suggests looping the cord around my neck. Nope. Too strange.

"Just let me hold it," I say, reaching for the mike.

Lise has the reflexes of a cobra. She snatches it from my right hand and puts it in my left. That way, she explains, viewers will see my wedding ring and instinctively know that this is not just some twisted way for me to meet women.

The sound guy leads me out to the spot where I'll be sitting. It's blindingly bright in here and I'm getting more anxious by the second. Late last night I realized I had better let my board of directors know what I'd be doing, so I sent them all an e-mail. I was clearly not asking for permission, and some boards would probably resent that. If I had proposed something like this at General Mills or most of the other companies I've worked at, they would have wrapped me in a straitjacket and taken me away. But in the Internet world we move boldly, and above all we move quickly. Seek forgiveness, not permission, we always say.

The combination of the cold studio air and the sweat tsunami I'm generating is giving me the chills. I can see myself in the monitor and I look even more naked than I feel. I look at Lise and mumble furtively: "Is this gonna be okay?" She smiles back weakly and says, "Too late now, buddy." I'm mentally calculating what I'll tell my family and friends if this bombs. What if the stock collapses because people see this and think I'm not a serious enough CEO? The interviewer's voice in my earpiece startles me back to the moment. (Visit www.10secondmanager.com to see the now famous, near-naked visual!)

The first question is, of course, why I've chosen to appear half-naked. I talk about the Naked Man commercial (in which a man works in his home office completely naked, much to the consternation of his neighbors and the UPS delivery man) and how it communicates the power of downloading software digitally. I talk about how I'm the only Internet CEO who has a product that you can get at home without even having to get dressed. The whole reason I came here was to get the digital download message out and tie it to the Naked Man commercial. Now that I've done that, I feel my entire body relaxing. Surprising even me, the interviewer doesn't mention my lack of clothes again.

After the show, I check my e-mail and my voice mail. Every one of our directors has registered a positive, supportive message. In the next week, there are dozens of media "pickups," from television news and every form of print media, from *USA Today* and *Fort Worth StarTelegram* to *Federal Computer Week* and the *London Daily Telegraph*. Salon.com, commentators on Internet culture, called me a "pasty, shameless

CEO." But so what? Our goal was to get the word out and traffic site up. About 22.6 million people were "exposed" to digital downloading thanks to that appearance. Traffic on the site zoomed way up. We did the job.

So why should you care about me walking around in my shorts on television? I'm not trying to prove how brave I was or what a stud I am. What I want to share is the importance of establishing and building your company into a brand and aggressively getting the message out about what your brand means.

A lot of high-tech people don't understand branding. And a lot of brand people don't understand high tech, especially the Internet. The two worlds do overlap, though, and the space where they do is where fortunes are made. The pace there is fast and furious; it's literally kill or be killed. Jeff Bezos saw the opportunities right from the beginning and so did the guys and gals behind E*Trade, eToys, Yahoo!, and every other successful site on the Internet. AOL figured it out, too, and pulled a nimble judo move on Silicon Valley. AOL grabbed the masses by trumpeting its simplicity and ease of use while Netscape and others were trying to appeal to the technogeeks. In a complicated, high-tech world, the AOL brand told millions of people that there was a place for those of us who'd never heard of Usenet and didn't have a clue about bandwidth but wanted to feel connected, wanted to feel cool. Now AOL owns Netscape.

Doing business on the Internet today is not, if you'll pardon the pun, a dress rehearsal. Key markets are getting divvied up like mining claims during the Gold Rush. If you're going to succeed, you'll need to capture market share, but market share's not enough. You must also grab consumer mind share, meaning that when consumers need something, your company (and your brand) is the first thing that pops into their heads. (Adding a room to your house? Home Depot. Need your morning coffee fix? Starbucks. Got a paper cut? Band-Aid.) And finally, you'll need financial market mind share (meaning that investors see you as a growing power and are bullish on your stock), and competitor fear share (everyone else in your category is running scared).

Some of the most popular brands have gone one step farther and have become almost generic terms. Xerox, Kleenex, and others undoubtedly have armies of overpaid lawyers who do nothing all day long but write snooty letters arguing that Xerox is not synonymous with copying and Kleenex is not synonymous with tissue. Most people, though, would kill for that kind of branding problem. I've heard people say they "just Amazon it" if they need a book quickly. There's nothing I would have liked better than to hear somebody suggest you "Beyond it" if you need software.

The following ten tips are the absolute essentials for feeding, watering, massaging, and cultivating your own brand. You may not end up as recognizable as McDonalds or Kleenex, but if you're lucky you won't have to take your clothes off.

1. Figure out how to position yourself. On the Internet, branding isn't just the name of the game, it *is* the game. And the struggle to establish it starts at the very beginning, with the business sector and the core brand attributes you choose. To have a successful site you have to give consumers enough added value to overcome the incredible hassles of the Internet itself. Why should they have to deal with slow modems, random disconnects, occasional computer crashes, and having to wait at least a day to get something they order from you, when they can just go into a store, squeeze the Charmin, and walk out with it?

It's critical to focus on the unmet needs of customers when picking the category you want to be in. Ask yourself (or, better yet, ask prospective customers) what frustrates them about the way they currently buy what you're thinking of selling. What causes them pain and aggravation? How can you save them time and make their lives easier?

Beyond.com banked on the misery most people feel when they have to get into their car and go to a software store. Instead of parking hassles, long lines, and poorly trained employees, Beyond.com offers superior helpfulness, selection, convenience, and better pricing. What software buyers really want to know is, "What works on my computer . . . with my operating system . . . with my current programs . . . and does what I want it to do?" Now, I'm sure that if they go to their local store on the right day and find the right employee at the right times, they'll get an answer to those questions. But what are their odds of hitting the right day? Better than hitting the right lottery number? Not by much. Using the Internet Beyond.com can make sure it's the right day every day. Using the Internet Beyond.com can streamline the process, communicate with your computer and find out exactly what programs you're already running and offer customized suggestions for what would be the best option for the new task you want to do. And to top it off, you can have your software cheaper and faster than at your local store by digitally downloading it.

Every category has unmet needs—areas where customers are frustrated with their current options. If you can identify them and be the first one to satisfy those needs on the Internet, you'll be able to pull off a coup similar to what Amazon did in the book business and what Beyond.com did to the software business.

While you're doing your research on your market sector, be sure to focus on competitive concentration. Ask yourself how many competitors account for 80 percent of the category's total volume? If it's only a few, that's bad news—it's going to be hard to break in because they've already got most of the customers. But if there are hundreds of competitors, that means there's a lot of unmet demand out there. Sounds counterintuitive (Why get into a market where you have to fight with a bunch of other people when you can get into one with only a few?) but it's true.

Long before Jeff came along, Barnes & Noble and Borders were big-name players in the bookstore world. But as big as they were, they had a combined market share of only about 30 percent. That, plus the existence of so many thousands of competitors, was proof that plenty of customers weren't relying on Barnes & Noble or Borders to fill all their book needs. A typical Barnes & Noble store might have 100,000 individual titles (the biggest has about 250,000), but that's just a small fraction of all the books customers might be looking for. Ingram, the largest book distributor, carries around 400,000 individual titles. And if you add in backlist (noncurrent), out-of-print, and rare books, you're looking at over 4 million titles. And at any given moment there's probably someone out there looking for every single one of them. Barnes & Noble couldn't possibly stock those additional 3.9 million books in each of their physical stores. But with a virtual store it would be no problem. And that's exactly why Jeff Bezos decided to go into the book business instead of some other.

EToys is another company that took advantage of a huge but fragmented market. By the time Toys 'R' Us reacted and launched their own e-commerce site, it was too late. EToys was the first mover and had already established themselves as the Internet brand. Agency.com, Doubleclick, and Flycast all did the same thing in the advertising business. All three have built up huge businesses in a very short period of time. And Blue Mountain Arts was the first Internet mover into the enormous greeting card business, and it survives on word of mouth (you send a card, you get one back). They actually have more traffic than Amazon.com and were bought by Excite@ Home for nearly $1 billion.

If you already have an established brand, it's difficult to link your e-commerce and real-world businesses. Or, as we say in the Valley, "bricks and clicks don't work." In the computer business, for example, Dell is far better situated on-line than most of the other computer .com sites, such as IBM.com. The problem is "channel conflict." Existing sales channels (the retailers who stock IBM products) don't like having to compete with a supplier who sells direct. And they especially don't like when the supplier is undercutting their prices.

Egghead was one of the first brick-and-mortar-only companies to "relocate" from land-based to web-based. It was the only way they could survive. I expect that more and more brick-and-mortar retailers will make the transition as well.

Some companies have figured out how to run Internet and brick-and-mortar operations successfully. Drugstore giant Rite-Aid is involved with Drugstore.com, which will give customers the additional option of ordering on-line and picking up at their local store. And then of course there's Barnes & Noble, which isn't about to close their bookstores. What they did, however, was create a completely separate company (BN.com), take it public, and run it with a completely separate CEO and board. Perhaps more bricks-and-clicks successes will come along, but I believe that a clean slate is still the best beginning.

2. **Choose the right name.** I'm often asked by industry experts if a brand name is really important on the Internet. Absolutely. In fact, I think brand names on the Internet are more important than they are off! In the physical world, brand names like Coca-Cola and McDonald's help consumers narrow down thousands of options to just a few with visual reminders, like distinctive red cans or golden arches. On the Internet there aren't any cans or arches. Your name is the only thing that separates your site from the nearly one billion others out there. If anyone is going to buy from you, they have to know your brand name—and know how to spell it—so they can type it into their web browser.

Internet names should be short, easy to spell, and start

toward the front of the alphabet, largely because search engines often alphabetize search results and you want to be at the top of the list. Think of Amazon, eToys, eBay, and iVillage, for example. Some of the best brick-and-mortar brands have had trouble making the transition to the Internet because they didn't follow this rule. Take Barnes & Noble again. They have a classy, familiar, solid-sounding brand name, but do you write out the "and" or can you use "&" instead? Is it Barns or Barnes? Are there spaces between the words or is it all one lump? These questions might sound silly, but if a customer can't find your site the first time he tries, chances are he'll move on to someone else's. It's a lot less confusing now that they've changed to BN.com.

There are generally two ways to come up with a name. The first is to pick an existing word that captures the image you're trying to present. Amazon, for example, conjures up images of something huge and majestic, which is exactly what the company wants. According to market research, people associate the word *Beyond* with the future, with aspirations, with technology, with hope. We chose the name Beyond.com because these are great attributes to attach to software reselling and they are the same "personality" characteristics that we were striving to get across in our advertising and public relations. The other option is to come up with a fanciful word or phrase and give it a new meaning. Yahoo! and Nike did this wonderfully; neither word really means anything, but they've both got a lot of personality.

Watch out, though. Plenty of companies have made major name-selection blunders. The Mining Company was a very nice search engine and their tag was that they gave you more personal service because they had real people who "mined the web" to find your answer. A good concept, but when people heard the name Mining Company they thought of coal or iron or 3M (Minnesota Mining and Manufacturing). Wisely, they changed their name to About.com. Their new slogan—"just about everything"—is a lot easier to remember and really projects the image that you'll be able to find everything you're searching for.

Cyberian Outpost is another example of a name gone wrong. (They're the people behind the gerbil commercials we talked about earlier.) When you first hear the name Cyberian Outpost, what business do you think they're in? And would you have any idea that it was Cyberian and not Siberian? No one else did either, so they eventually dropped the Cyberian altogether.

Before Beyond.com, the company was Software.net, which I thought was a pretty good name—software on the net—easy to remember, easy to spell. The problem was that customers couldn't tell us from Software.com or Anysoft or any of the other soft names out there. Before we changed the name we conducted some customer surveys and found that even people who had bought from us had no idea who we were or how they'd stumbled onto our site in the first place.

If your business already has an established name that fits the criteria above, take advantage of your name recognition and keep using it. But if your company name is unwieldy or boring, consider changing it. Abercrombie and Fitch wisely changed their on-line name to Abercrombie.com (another case of "&" or "and," three words or one).

Even if you have a big name in your industry, you still might want to make some subtle changes when you get onto the web. Kbkids.com, for example, is the product of the marriage of brainplay.com and Consolidated Stores, which own thirteen hundred K*B Toys stores. They're taking advantage of the big K*B name but there's enough of a distinction so it's clear that Kbkids.com is a separate business.

And if it isn't already obvious, be sure to make your URL (your Internet address) the same as your company name. (Think of Amazon.com, Beyond.com, ParentsPlace.com—the ".com" is actually part of the name.) Before the awkwardly named Planning and Architecture Internet Resource Center, its URL was an impossible to remember www.arch. buffalo.edu/pairc. Now it's *www.Cyburbia.org.*

3. **Create the right image.** Before Amazon.com was very well known, people who visited the site and who read the early articles about this growing company in the Northwest had the impression that we were a bunch of friendly out-doorsy folks in Eddie Bauer plaid shirts and khakis cheerfully packing boxes as fast as we could so you got that book you wanted. We portrayed ourselves as happy—but somewhat surprised—at our own success and promised that we'd stop at absolutely nothing to make you happy.

Reality and the image you create don't have to be—and rarely are—identical. There are plenty of great people at Amazon, and they are passionate about customer service. But that's where the similarities between reality and image end. The pace is far from casual and no one's sitting around thinking about fly-fishing or cross-country skiing. They're working incredibly hard, relentlessly crunching numbers, looking for competitive advantages and leverage in high-wire negotiations, pushing and pushing to make everything happen faster than seems humanly possible. If you wandered into the warehouse, instead of peaceful, smiling people in Eddie Bauer shirts, you'd bump into a bunch of cynical, headphone wearing Gen-X kids with multiple tattoos and body piercings moving books and packing boxes.

So think about the image you want to present to your prospective customers and make sure everything you do—from advertising to customer service to the way you design your site—reinforces your brand image. Part of Yahoo!'s image, for example, is based on speed. Their commercials are fast and their site itself is ruthlessly fast. They could fill their pages with eye-popping graphics, video clips, or funny voices, but all that would make the site run slower, which would be completely contrary to their image.

One warning: a lot of companies these days try to attract

attention by creating a wacky, wild, creative, fun image. I think
Beyond.com did that pretty successfully with the Naked Man
campaign. (And no, people at Beyond.com are not running
around the office naked.) But it's not that easy to pull off; too
many companies have nearly died trying. Outpost's gerbil commercials were certainly wacky, wild, and creative. But they were
so shocking that the image they ultimately gave was unpre-
dictable and unstable instead of fun. Instability isn't a quality
customers are looking for when they're deciding whether or
not they want to have a relationship with you.

AOL has built its image on being easy to use, something
that's extremely important to the 99 percent of the world
that's technically challenged. And eToys projects an image of
being new, young, and a lot more fun than Toys 'R' Us. Established companies can actually take advantage of the Internet
to revamp their image. Before they became Abercrombie.com,
Abercrombie & Fitch had a pretty stodgy image. Now it's cool,
hip, fresh.

In general, people who shop on-line do so for convenience, selection, price, and helpfulness—in that order. But
that order can shift, depending on the category. With software, for example, helpfulness is the top reason. People are
overwhelmed and don't consider themselves capable of making the right choice on their own. The same thing is probably
true for people who buy wine on-line.

4. **Link your image and your name.** Think of your
brand name as an empty vessel into which you pour your
image. The two can't really exist independently. Your name
isn't worth much without an image for people to relate to, and
your image is useless without a name to associate it with. To
be most successful, vessel and contents, image and name
should be in the same place at the same time.

McDonald's does this incredibly well with its golden
arches. And Coca-Cola has its famous curvy Coke glass, which

it puts everywhere—even on its cans. Still, as painfully simple as it sounds to link your image and your name, it's surprisingly tricky.

Think about the Energizer Bunny. It's a great concept with very memorable commercials. But quick, do you know whether it's Duracell or Eveready? Are you sure? Alka-Seltzer had a similar problem when they launched their *plop plop, fizz fizz* campaign. People all over the country were humming the tune all day long, but surveys showed that almost no one could recall the product being advertised.

On the Internet, however, most businesses haven't been around long enough to develop visual corporate images like golden arches and curvy glasses. We have to rely on name recognition and the mental image that name evokes.

5. **Fish where the fish are.** In the physical world, stores are extremely concerned about customer counts—the more people who come in, the better chance a store has of making a sale. It's the same on the Internet. And just like in real estate, a large component of a physical store's success is location, location, location. Again, it's the same on the Internet. Sort of. Instead of a physical location, Internet companies need to "set up shop" in consumers' minds (through advertising and promotion), on their computers (in their "favorite site" links), and on popular sites where their product is relevant. These links—ads, buttons, banners, and other "click here" spots that take consumers from wherever they are to your site—are the Internet equivalent of building your physical store on a busy main street. The Internet also offers a few distinct advantages over physical stores: you don't have the huge expenses associated with leasing or constructing or buying a store. And best of all, you can "build" an infinite number of entrances to your store and you can put them anywhere your target audience is likely to hang out.

Where you build those entrances is, of course, going to

depend on the kind of business you're in. But the basic rule is that you want to establish links to your site from other high-traffic sites that will attract a likely audience for your products or services.

No one has put up more links more effectively than Amazon. Just about every book author in the country who has a website has it linked to Amazon. It's called their "Associates program" and Amazon pays a commission to the referring website for every sale. Many organizations have also become Associates, offering their members and other visitors the chance to buy specific books from their "bookstore," which just happens to be linked to Amazon. As a result, Amazon has highly targeted links on thousands of pages all over the web.

Setting up your own affiliate program isn't that hard. It's really all about doing exactly what Amazon does—encouraging people who already have an interest in your products or services to refer others to your website by paying them a commission on sales. The best way to sign up affiliates is to put up a notice on your home page letting people know that they can make money by sending customers your way. If you don't want to do all this yourself, you can always outsource the whole thing to one of a number of companies, such as Adweb1 (Adweb1.com).

Be aware that putting up links is going to cost you. Doing business on the Internet allows you to instantly track a number of essential statistics that traditional businesses have virtually no way of ever acquiring. You'll be able to track the percentage of site visitors who buy something, how much the average transaction is, what percentage of customers come back to buy again and how often, and the exact number of visitors coming to your site from every link you set up. With all that information it's easy to put a precise dollar value on each new visitor. Each portal or traffic source, however, will yield a different value. This is because each portal has different demographics, which means that visitors from one may be more or less likely to buy than visitors from another.

6.   **Advertise and publicize.** It's critical in the early days of establishing your brand to get your message "above the buzz"—into the hearts and minds and watercooler conversations of as many people as possible as quickly as possible. If at least 10 percent of your target audience doesn't know who you are, your chances of succeeding are pretty slim. Television, with its penetration into nearly 100 percent of American homes, boosts your chances more than any other medium.

Radio, of course, is still a good option, but it can reach only 35 to 40 percent of the total market. And while hearing your company's name on the radio is good—Amazon had a lot of success with its "where can we find a place big enough to put 2.5 million books" radio campaign—seeing it is better. Hearing and seeing it at the same time, though, is the best of all because it more than doubles your chances of people remembering your name. Since that's exactly what potential customers have to do to get to your site, you should be doing anything you can to etch your name into their brains.

Television advertising is expensive, though, and is well beyond the reach of most smaller companies. If you can't afford to televise your image, all is not lost—not by any means. First, start with radio. It's pretty cheap and you can still reach a lot of people. Second, work extra hard to establish links to your site from high-traffic sites where your target customers are hanging out.

If you can't do any of these, you absolutely must hire yourself a publicist or public relations director. The media loves a good .com story—especially if it's David vs. Goliath—but you've got to get the word out.

The publicist for the folks who started ParentsPlace.com (a huge parenting site now owned by iVillage) was able to get ParentsPlace.com mentioned in newspaper, magazine, and television stories all across the country—coverage and publicity they never would have been able to afford. The publicist, however, was their single biggest expense—more than salaries, equipment, and overhead.

A good rule of thumb with the press is to actively sell your story—but be wary of stories that they come to you with! Many reporters have a story in mind before they contact you and you may be pre-cast as hero—or villain. Listen closely to the story they are trying to write before you agree to participate.

And finally, focus on serving your customer every way you can. As we discussed, the single biggest draw to your site is going to be word-of-mouth recommendations. Your goal is to make everyone who visits your site an evangelist.

7. **Hire some food guys.** The message here is that after the CEO, CTO, and CIO, the head of marketing is the most valuable guy in the company, and you'd better find someone good to fill the slot. If you get the opportunity to hire some food marketers you should jump at the chance. Okay, okay, you don't have to limit yourself to only food companies. But given my background (at Kraft Foods and Dreyer's/Edy's Grand Ice Cream), I guess I'm a little partial.

Big-name consumer goods companies such as Kraft, Procter & Gamble, Frito-Lay, Pepsi, and Coke usually hire MBAs from top schools and put them through marketing boot camp. Sometimes, though, they'll hire a marketing or business undergrad. New hires get rigorous training in brand positioning, consumer research, promotions, and advertising. They also get a ton of experience in one of the most competitive markets out there. It's a market in which a decimal-point difference in the cost of goods can be worth millions of dollars and a decimal-point difference in market share can be worth even more. These guys have to figure out every possible way to make their products stand out from the thirty thousand others on the shelves in every grocery store.

On the Internet, your marketing department's primary goal is to get your site to stand out from a billion others, and you want someone with the skills to do that. Jeff Bezos says that marketing is a lot harder than high-level computer programming. Coming from him, that's an incredible compliment.

Ideally, you'd hire a top-performing marketing VP away from another Internet company. But there aren't enough people like that to go around, and I can guarantee you that finding a good marketing VP is probably the toughest search in Silicon Valley; they're arguably as hard to find as CTOs, CIOs, or even CEOs. As a result, people outside the Valley are raiding consumer-goods companies left and right. I brought people from Unilever, Clorox, Quaker Oats, and others into Beyond.com. The fact is that anyone with a classic consumer-goods background—whether it's selling household cleaners, GM cars, or Johnson & Johnson baby shampoo—is worth a long, hard look.

If your budget won't allow someone with a consumer-goods "pedigree," there are a lot of quality people working in direct marketing, such as catalog and mail-order sales. AOL hired a lot of people like this to work on their incredibly successful "fifty (or one hundred or five hundred) free hours" campaigns.

Keep in mind, though, that while someone with a solid consumer-goods background with a major company is almost guaranteed to act smart, there's no guarantee that he or she will act fast. So before you hire anyone, go back and reread "Hire Fast People," in Chapter 1.

If your business isn't yet at the stage where you can afford a top consumer-goods refugee, look for candidates with a serious background in business development, public relations, and advertising. Building your brand is your company's main concern, and an incredibly expensive one at that. So hire the absolute best person you can afford. These on-line categories are forming very quickly—usually in eighteen to twenty-four months—and your marketing VP must be someone who has the creativity and vision to take you to the top and keep you there. Skimping on a marketing guy will cost you in the long run no matter what size your company is now and no matter what size you want it to be in the future.

⑧. **Ignore the message boards and chat rooms.** This may sound like a contradiction to what we talked about in relation to customer feedback, but it's not. What you have to know about message boards is that most of the people who post on them are not your customers. And they're not your friends. They're self-interested people who have hidden biases and agendas. They're day-traders and short-sellers, deranged minds, and people who are trying to drive your company's stock or your image one way or the other. (Message boards are basically electronic versions of bathroom graffiti—someone posts a comment and others post responses. There's no live interaction. Chat rooms, on the other hand, are like an old-time party-line telephone—a bunch of people in a virtual room talking at the same time about a particular topic.)

So why should you pay any attention to a message board? First of all, a lot of the major websites display stock quotes and have message board or chat room links right next to them. It's incredibly easy to click—just to see what people are talking about. A lot of employees do this. Second, message boards are so popular that even if you don't go into one, I can guarantee you that some of your friends, family, and employees will, and they'll e-mail you little snippets of the discussions they're reading. It's awfully tempting—especially if you read something that's not true—to want to post a response to straighten everyone out.

In a debate, the person with the mike always wins. On a message board you don't have the mike, they do. Once you post something it's there forever. Hundreds of people could respond to what you say and hundreds more could respond to those responses, putting a completely different spin on your words and never giving you a chance to explain. You simply can't win. You're only one of potentially thousands of people posting. But you're a very prestigious one. And by posting, you're giving these people credibility when you really should be staying as far away from them as possible. Here's why:

▷   You're putting things in writing. If you are an executive, you always represent your company—nothing you say is truly off the record. So even though a message board might seem informal, whatever you type in is your company's official written position. Your annual reports, your website content, and even your press releases probably go through some kind of legal review (if they don't, they should). Everything else you write should be subjected to the same scrutiny. Without a legal review, anything you write—even if it's a typo—could be distorted or misconstrued and passed all over the world. By the time you wake up the next morning your stock might be in the tank. Hardly seems worth the risk, does it?

▷   You could get yourself into trouble with the Security and Exchange Commission (SEC). As a public company, it's illegal to selectively disclose material company information. When you're posting something on a message board or in a chat room answering questions, responding to accusations, or defending your actions, you might inadvertently reveal something you shouldn't. Might be something minor or it might not. Either way it could land you in trouble.

▷   If you're not convinced and you can't resist hearing what people are saying, at least log in under an alias and don't say a word. It's the closest you'll ever come to being a fly on the wall and you might actually learn something. People in a chat room after my boxers-only CNBC stint made two suggestions: (1) get that guy out of the Internet company and out into the sun!; and (2) fire the male CEO, get a female!

9.   **Earn your customers' trust.** People want as much control over their lives as they possibly can have. When it comes to your site, they want to select which—if any—newsletters or product reminders or updates they get and how often. They want to be able to change their credit card number, their address, and their password. The good news is that this is extremely easy to do on most e-commerce sites. The even better news is that doing so will save you money and make your customers more committed and more loyal.

But the bad news is that because e-commerce companies have so much information on their customers (address, credit card number, product preference, how much they spend, etc.), there are tremendous opportunities for abuse. And abusing a customer's trust is just about the best way to lose him.

When I was at Amazon we did a major site update and wanted to send out a mailing to everyone who'd ever been a customer and invite them back. I drafted a short letter but our tech department refused to send it out. "It's spam," they said. "The customers didn't ask to be e-mailed and we shouldn't send them anything." Naturally, Jeff and I disagreed with the techies. He reminded them that the way we got customers' e-mail addresses in the first place was because they'd done business with us. More important, when they'd first visited the site we'd given them a chance to check a box and opt out of receiving any mailings from us. We were respecting that choice. He then pulled out an e-mail solicitation he'd received from some porn site. "This is spam," he said. "I've never done business with these people. They bought my name under false pretenses and they're sending me crap I didn't ask for."

He was right. But while most customers appreciate hearing your news, there's always a fraction of a percent of people who get truly irate at getting a mass e-mail. This mailing didn't generate any more business than the expected percentage.

Every legitimate Internet company now gives visitors or customers the option to opt out by checking a box or boxes indicating the kind of information—if any—they want to get from you. If they don't specifically opt out, we assumed that they're in. So when collecting names, be completely up front about exactly what you're doing. Let anyone who visits your site know that you'd like to send them occasional notifi-cations of new products or site features. You can even en-courage people to give you their addresses by having a sweepstakes or contest. But whatever you do, make sure they have the option to opt out and make it easy to do so. And if they do, keep your promise and don't send them anything. It's all part of the trust thing.

_10._ **Think globally.** Even though it's a mostly American phenomenon, the Internet offers incredible opportunities to take your brand global. Coke, for example, is probably the most recognized brand in the world. Nike and Microsoft are certainly everywhere in industrialized countries. And Michael Jordan, a kind of one-person brand, has better recognition in some countries than even the presidents of those countries!

But before you solidify your final brand and image, make sure you've considered how they'll play in the rest of the world. Here are two big factors to consider:

▷ **Get international trademarks.** By not registering your brand name in other countries, you're leaving the door open for some fast-acting entrepreneur. This means that if you ever decide to expand overseas, you might find that someone else is riding high on your brand identity and the goodwill you worked so hard to achieve. If you decide to do business in that country, it could cost you big bucks to buy the rights to your own name. This is exactly what happened to Amazon.com in Greece, where some clever people registered Amazon.gr (the Greek equivalent of .com) and Amazon had to sue to get their own name back.

This is basically the same thing "cybersquatters" do here when they register Internet domain names that are identical to or confusingly similar to existing company names or the names of famous people, hoping to sell them later. Microsoft recently prevailed against two guys who had registered microsoftwindows.com and microsoftoffice.com. And Avon was successfully able to regain the rights to avon.com. They won, but it wasn't cheap.

▷ **Check your translations.** In Chinese, Kentucky Fried Chicken's slogan, "finger-lickin' good," came out as "eat your fingers off." Ford executives spent a long time scratching their heads trying to figure out why the Pinto was a complete flop in Brazil. Then someone told them that *pinto* was Brazilian slang for "tiny male genitals." And the folks at Gerber didn't know that because of high illiteracy rates in some African countries, pictures on the outside of packages are always representative of what's inside. No surprise, then, that customers were more than a little repelled by that cute baby on the baby food labels. The marketing world—and the Internet—is filled with blunders like these that could have been avoided if the company had spent a few more minutes checking things out. So spend a little time and you'll keep yourself from falling into branding hell.

For more tips on branding—and to offer your own tips—visit *www.10secondmanager.com/branding.*

SURVIVING THE
INVESTMENT JUNGLE

I f your schedule is anything like mine, there's a pretty good chance that you're reading this book on a plane en route to some kind of investor meeting. In 1998 and 1999, I spent about a third of my time flying all over the country meeting with investment firms, speaking at investor conferences, and hosting investors who made the trek to our Silicon Valley headquarters. It's a ritual that all public Internet CEOs must go through during the unending process of placating institutional investors who have the power to add—or subtract—millions from your company's valuation literally overnight.

These big financing trips—having to do with initial public offerings (IPOs) and secondary offerings—usually last about three weeks at a time and include at least twenty-one cities, sometimes as many as three in a day. I sometimes find these trips, or at least parts of them, exhilarating (meeting with someone who manages billions of dollars of other people's money is always a kick) and intellectually stimulating (chatting about technology and the future of the Internet with some of the world's brightest people may be a little intimidating but it sure is fun).

Just about every investor tour makes the same rounds: Janus in Denver, Fidelity in Boston, J.P. Morgan in New York, AmEx in Minneapolis, and many others. And let's not forget about the pilgrimages to that powerful independent fund manager, Glenn Doshay, at his palace in the hills above San Diego.

Now, although this chapter is supposedly focusing on how Internet companies should deal with investors, the information here applies equally well to a variety of other business situations you might find yourself in. You could be doing a media interview, for example, or you could be trying to raise money to build new stores and expand your physical-world presence; you might be in the process of dragging your company, kicking and screaming, into the Internet age, or you might be meeting with your bosses or your company's finance committee trying to convince them to commit some money to an important project. These tips should help you handle any of these situations.

The finance world is a jungle. But no matter where you go or what you're going there for (as long as it's money), you'll find that the animals who inhabit this jungle fall into several distinct categories. So before we start hacking through the underbrush, let's take a look at who they are.

▷ **The young.** It's like some kind of nightmare: you've spent weeks preparing your big presentation and you walk into a conference room feeling confident and ready to go. The big leather chair slowly spins around and you see that the person in it, the person you're making your pitch to, is a seven-year-old.

Okay, you're not really ever going to have a meeting with a seven-year-old. But the fact is that some of these investors *are* very young, probably in their mid-twenties, and they often look even younger. They may seem naïve and they probably don't have a lot of real-life work experience, but don't underestimate them. They're where they are because they're smart. And as incredibly ironic as it is, your company's future, your employees' future, and possibly even your own financial security hang on your ability to impress them.

▷   **The innocent.** Over the past year, growth in Internet stocks has been so spectacular that institutional investors can no longer ignore them. Doing so increases the risk that their portfolios will underperform the market, which is the investment community's equivalent of getting an "F" on a report card.

So every once in a while you'll find yourself in a meeting with an investor who really needs to take e-Commerce 101. "I'm new to the firm and we're considering picking up some Internet stocks in the next year and I'd love to hear about your company," they'll say with a big grin on their fresh faces. "Now, what do you guys do again?" You might also get the same questions from a journalist who isn't quite clear what you do.

When you hear a question like that your first reaction might be to say something nasty or condescending and storm out in a huff. Don't. Even though the guy is wasting your time, and even though he could get himself up to speed by reading your prospectus, these meetings are important. Yes, you're giving up a little (okay, a lot) of your time, but the Internet virgin sitting across the conference table from you today could be a rising star, a guy you're going to be glad you know in a few months or years. Consider it an investment in your own future and be gentle.

▷   **The Mutt 'n' Jeff team.** In some meetings you'll be
double-teamed by an analyst and a fund manager. From
the minute the meeting starts, it's clear that they know a
lot about your business. They'll compliment you up and
down, tell you what a great company you have, and how
they've been keeping an eye on you for a long time.
They'll make you feel so comfortable and they'll seem
like such big fans that you'll start to relax. You'll let
down your guard.

It's right about then—and you might not even
notice this—that the dynamic changes. They'll turn into
Mutt and Jeff, two guys with very different agendas. The
analyst will ask you all sorts of provocative questions. He
wants to know your earnings per share, your revenues,
your margins, your break-even point, and every other
number he can get. He's basically building a financial
model of your business right before your eyes. The fund
manager, on the other hand, isn't really paying much
attention to what you say—or at least not to the *words*
you say. He's watching your hands and feet and the way
you stand. He's made a science of reading body language
and he's looking for subtle, almost unconscious tips—
facial tics, sweaty upper lips, stuttering, hemming and
hawing—that might indicate that things aren't as rosy as
you're painting them. He wants to know whether you
really believe what you're saying, because he has to take
your company to the rest of the firm and try to convince
them to jump on your bandwagon.

In a sense, meetings like these are a test of both the
substance and the form of your presentation. You can't
win on one and not the other. Know your stuff and give
clear, honest answers and you won't have anything to
worry about.

▷   **The fleecers.** You'll start your meeting calmly with
one or two investors. Then, five minutes in, several

distinguished-looking gentlemen will drop by. They're usually principles in the firm (there's just something about the way they look that gives that away; in Boston, for some reason, they always seem to be wearing bow ties). Sometimes you're introduced to them, sometimes not. Either way, they'll repeatedly interrupt your presentation with questions. When at Beyond.com, I remember one string of queries on the same topic. Where are your servers? Ours happened to be at a local firm, Exodus. Are you happy with Exodus? Do you think you'll be with them a year from now? What do you think of Abovenet [Exodus's East Coast competitor]? Where do you see server-hosting pricing over the next two to three years? Which portals are working for you? Which will be around in three years?

All these questions may seem pertinent to your presentation, and that's where you'll get tripped up. What's really happening is that they're pumping you for information they can use to guide their entire Internet portfolio. Sometimes they'll reword a question three or four times, trying to confuse you into answering something you don't want to. They may try to entice you to give up information by sprinkling around interesting tidbits about other Internet companies. But don't think that the information flow is a one-way street. Whatever information you share with them will be passed on to everyone else they meet in conferences just like this one. (I've picked up a lot of excellent information on competitors in these meetings.) So be careful which questions you answer and how you answer them. And be especially careful if you're dealing with anyone from the media. We'll talk more about what you should and shouldn't say in situations like these.

▷ **Those who get it.** These are the guys I love to work with. They're up on the category, they're up on our company, and they can't wait to learn more. When I was on road shows for Beyond.com, I'd hear: "Okay, we know you're the first mover in a $100 billion software category that's going on-line faster than any other category on the Internet. And we know you're going to grab as much as 35 percent of the category in the next three to four years. But what I really want to know is specifically what you're going to do to preserve and extend that lead." These folks are the super-investors; they have minds like supercomputers and are capable of quickly processing the key success factors (category, competitor, customer, management team, proprietary technology). They're also incredible forward thinkers: I would be talking to them about software and they would be talking about some kind of new satellite technology and how it'll change the world. They're also great at multi-tasking: they can be scanning the key pages of your prospectus, flipping back and forth between charts showing your accumulated debt and your accounts receivables, and asking you rapid-fire questions about your stock options and your international plans—all at the same time.

You can learn a huge amount in these meetings by listening to what they have to say and paying attention to the kinds of questions they ask. But don't be afraid to ask them a few questions, too. They may have some great ideas on how to improve your business or on how some future technologies might affect it. Every time I have a meeting with guys like this, I leave feeling stimulated and excited about technology and how we're part of a huge change for a better, more empowering world.

▷ **Those who sort of get it but don't want to believe it.** It's easy to understand how the public might not understand why Internet companies have such incredibly high valuations—after all, most of them have yet to show a profit. But people have still paid billions for their stock. Amazon and eToys are just two examples. You'd expect portfolio managers to be a little more sophisticated. One of the basic rules is that the right price is whatever the market will bear. Yet there's a whole class of them who take high Internet valuations as a personal affront and act as though it's up to them to do something to correct this terrible injustice.

During Beyond.com's IPO tour, one investor I met with laid into me hard. "You mean that my colleagues and I are paying you $50 million so that you can turn around and give AOL $21 million of it over the next three and a half years?" he ranted. "That's going to help them report higher ad revenues and their stock will go up and this insanity will just keep going on and on." I tried to explain that I have a lot of experience with portal deals from my Amazon.com days and that I knew our AOL deal was a good one. But he kept shouting me down. "There's no profit here, there's no business here. This is criminal!"

Don't waste your time fighting with these guys. They just want to vent and there's probably not much you can do to convince them to see things your way. Just make your case as effectively as you can and be on your way.

▷ **Those who don't get it at all.** Sad to say, there are some investors out there who may simply never get this whole Internet thing. At Beyond.com, I remember one meeting with a very senior analyst at a well-known Boston investment bank. With its antique leather chairs and oak paneling, the conference room looked like something out of the nineteenth century. And so were the analyst's views. "Okay, young man," he said, lighting his cigar. "There are only three aspects to looking at any business: cash, accounts receivables, and inventory. Tell me how that works in your business."

I laughed and gave him the honest answers: "Little, none, and none," I said. "Internet companies deliberately lose money in their first few years to gain that all-important market share. We have positive working capital because we collect credit card payments before we ship anything, and we carry no inventory at all!"

The old-time, traditional income/receivables/inventory approach to analysis may work just fine for a physical retailer, but it doesn't apply at all to the Internet.

Now that you know about the animals you're likely to meet during your twenty-one-day safari through the investment jungle, pay close attention. The survival tips that follow could keep you and your company from getting severely injured. And again, these tips apply just as well to answering questions from a journalist and to almost any kind of financial meeting with anyone else, whether they're inside or outside your company.

1. **Practice makes perfect.** A newscaster friend once told me that the news consists of a handful of stories that repeat—sometimes with small variations—over and over and over. Someone's cat got stuck in a tree, a murderer escaped from prison, the stock market went up or down. . . . Cocktail party banter consists of the same eight or ten questions that cycle again and again: Where'd you grow up? Do you have any brothers and sisters? What do you do for a living? What do you think of the (fill in the name of your favorite local sports team)?

Well, in the investment jungle it's just about the same. No matter how many people you meet with or how bright they are, there are only about ten questions you'll ever get asked on your road show. For Beyond.com, they were: If you're downloading over the Internet, what do you do about the operating manual? (These days they're electronic.) How can people return the product? (Fax the company a letter certifying that they've removed it from their computer.) If it gets erased from my computer, how do I get a replacement copy? (You can download it again for free.) And What happens if I get disconnected in the middle of a download? (You log on again and our system automatically picks up where you left off.)

Your ten questions, of course, will be different. And there's a good chance you already know what they are—they're the ones you get from your friends and family when you tell them about your company. If you aren't sure, sit down with your banker or a friendly investor (or a whole bunch of them) and have them grill you before you hit the road.

People—even investors—ask questions that are based (or might be based) on their own personal experiences. Hone some killer answers to those potentially killer questions.

Sometimes, of course, you won't know what the ten questions (and you know this is just an estimate, right?) are until you're actually on the road. The first day or so out you'll feel a little unsure of yourself. But by the end of the second day you'll be in a groove and every question you get from then on will be one you've answered before.

2. **Take care of yourself.** Over the course of your business life you've probably spent more than a few days working a trade show. You stand on a hard floor for hours on end, give your pitch many times a day, and answer every question as if it's the first time you're hearing it instead of the sixty-seventh. Multiply that by three weeks and add in more plane rides than you've ever taken in your entire life and you get an idea of what a traditional investor road show is like. It's kind of like Bill Murray's life in the movie *Groundhog Day*.

The same day seems to repeat itself over and over and over and over.

Because the routine is basically the same every day, you won't have to do a lot of serious thinking, but you will have to deal with mind-numbing repetition and boredom as well as a sore back and swollen feet. Overall, it's far more of a physical challenge than an intellectual one. I don't want to sound like your mother, but if you're going to make it through this thing, you're going to have to take good care of yourself. On the physical side, that means starting to work out before the tour even starts, and eating right and taking advantage of all those hotel gyms while you're on the road. (You may not be able to work out much during the week, but at least try to fit in a moderate workout on the weekend.) And whatever you do, drink lots of water and get as much sleep as you can—even if it's on airplanes.

In *Groundhog Day*, Murray's character tries to come up with something every morning to make each day different from the last. Some of his solutions involve killing himself, but nothing keeps the days from repeating. Trying something new every day does at least make the days a little more interesting.

Suicide isn't really an option (although you'll probably contemplate it after a few days on the road). Try to come up with some fun things to help take the edge off the boredom. When Bill McKiernan and I were doing Beyond.com's pre-IPO show, we came up with some ridiculous ways to amuse ourselves. In the limo on the way to one of our presentations I told Bill that he'd have to use the word *Mesozoic* at least once during the meeting. The next day I had to figure out a way to slip in *protozoa*. As the road show went on and we got bolder (and giddier), we made it even harder by giving each other the word of the day just as we were about to start the conference. And finally, we started slipping each other notes during the actual presentation with the secret word. It wasn't much but it sure lightened things up a little. Amazingly, no one ever noticed.

3. **Know what not to say . . . (or, I could tell you, but then I'd have to kill you).** "Loose lips sink ships" was a popular phrase in World War II. When it comes to dealing with investors, that expression is just as valid today as it was during World War II. Whether you're dealing with the body readers, the fleecers, or even the people who get it, and no matter how comfortable you feel with a potential investor, be extremely careful about the kind of information you give out. Anything you divulge is out there forever; there's no way to take it back.

Basically, you don't want to give out any information you don't want your competitors—or anyone you might ever negotiate a deal with—to know. Once you give any of this information out there's no putting the genie back in the bottle. It'll be all over the investment community in a heartbeat, and because your competitors are meeting with the very same investors you are, they'll know about it soon afterward. So learn to keep your mouth shut.

Jeff Bezos at Amazon is absolutely maniacal about this. He believes—and he's absolutely right—that there are things he knows that no one else knows. For example, what's the best site to link with? Is it AOL? CNET? Yahoo!? Excite? Jeff, I, and a handful of other people know which links were the most fruitful for our category, and our competitors would kill to get that information. Chances are you also have got some secrets that could help your competitors.

If you're pushed, politely decline to share your secrets and say exactly why. Whoever you're talking to will be disappointed you didn't cave, but they'll also respect you. Would anyone really want to invest money in a company with a CEO who doesn't know when to keep his mouth shut and gives away important, proprietary information? Here are the kinds of things you want to keep to yourself:

▷   Anything about the "lifetime value" of your customers, which is how much revenue and margin each one should produce for you over at least the next five years. This information, in the hands of your next business partner, will set the floor price of your next deal!

▷   Anything specific about actual or projected advertising budgets or the effectiveness of your various advertising tools. It's probably okay to come up with a ranking (we spend the most on television, then radio, then print), but that's it. Do you really want to tell your competitors exactly how to maximize their advertising spending?

▷   How much you pay for key partnerships. Giving this information away completely undermines your negotiating position. If Yahoo! knows you're paying Excite@Home $10 per customer, they'll never accept $9.

▷   Any of your secrets on how to crush the competition. This could include technical modifications, alternate advertising strategies, and site navigational changes. If it worked for you it will probably work for others.

▷   Anything you've done that hasn't worked out especially well for the company. Knowing what mistakes to avoid will shorten your competitors' learning curve and give them a chance to catch up to you.

$4.$ **Know what it's okay to say.** Of course, you can't just go into an investor meeting and refuse to talk at all. But you're there to convince them that your company has momentum (with a capital M) and that their fund better get on board fast. For example, if you are in the e-commerce business, you should be prepared to talk about:

▷   The number of customers you currently have and/or expect to have.

▷   The percentage of your volume that comes from repeat customers.

▷   Total revenues and trends.

   ▷ Gross margin percentages and trends.
   ▷ Something sketchy about your average transaction size.

Remember, the SEC requires that any discussion of material information must be shared with all investors at the same time. However, SEC regulations don't necessarily stop aggressive investors from probing you for that information for their own purposes. So be wary. Not following these rules will get you skewered, plain and simple. Again, any information you give out is out forever, so be careful what you say.

5. **Sing momentum with a capital *M*.** The Internet (and any other business) story is all about who's going to be number one, especially in large, fast-growing categories. So, if you've got momentum in your category, start singing.

In the first verse, tell them how big your category is, how fast it's growing, how much of it is moving on-line (if you're not in an Internet business, skip that one), and how much of the market you can reasonably capture. Beyond.com's went something like this:

"The software category is going to be over $100 billion by 2002. It's growing at 17 percent a year, and by 2002, 35 percent of it will be on-line. That means we're competing in a $35 billion market. If we're wildly successful, we'll capture 80 percent market share, or $28 billion. If we're wildly unlucky, we'll get 20 percent of the market and that's still $7 billion."

In the second verse you tell them how you're going to keep your competitors from eroding your market share. Here's the one we used at Beyond.com:

"We control two factors that are barriers to entry for potential competitors: first, we're the brand leader right now, and that's a pretty big obstacle in itself; second, we have proprietary technology in our digital downloading that makes us run faster, smoother, and more profitably than anyone else out there. Sure, our competitors could replicate what we have, but by the time they did we'd be miles ahead again."

Sometimes, if you have any particularly good information, you can add a third verse. Beyond.com had a chance to do this when it bought BuyDirect.com. We went on the road a few months later and told everyone that we'd not only bought our top competitor, we'd also secured their marketing partners: CNET, ZDNet, Excite@Home, and Roadrunner. Combined with our partners, we'd secured all the major beachheads. There would be no stopping us now.

6.   Be honest. Bill McKiernan and I were in the lobby of a hotel in New York practicing our presentation when an old man came walking up. "Let me give you some advice," he said. "Just be honest." And he walked away. I have no idea who that guy was, but he was absolutely right. Investors want to know about your company, but they also want to know whether you're honest, confident, and capable. Do I trust putting my portfolio's money in this person?

If you don't know the answer to a question, say so. If you think you can track down the answer, offer to get back to them later. And if you do know the answer to a question but don't want to answer, tell them that, too.

7.   Dress the part. As I've said earlier, there is no dress code in the Internet world. In fact, if you come to work wearing a suit you might get thrown out of the building. But you need to remember that the Internet world isn't like the rest of the world. Jeans and a T-shirt may be fine in your office, but you'll need suits when you're dealing with investors.

Fashion and conservative approaches to financing in the investment world haven't changed much in the last hundred years. So be prepared. If you show up for an investor meeting without a power tie and a Brooks Brothers suit you run the risk that they'll think you're a bike messenger—and treat you accordingly.

A SPECIAL NOTE IF YOU'RE DEALING WITH EARLY INVESTORS

If you're still in the early stages of financing your company, the kinds of investors you'll be meeting will be somewhat different from those we talked about at the beginning of this chapter. As a general rule, you'll be dealing with the company founder's social network as well as friends and family.

In the first round of financing (Series A), some of these people will invest hundreds of thousands of dollars, others only $5,000 or $10,000. They don't want to give out too much money too soon—they want you to demonstrate that you can operate cost-effectively. And you don't want to give away too much of the company too cheap. If you value your company at $2 million, you might be willing to sell a 10 percent stake for $200,000, enough to hire the basic staff you need to get the business off the ground. Six to nine months later, if your business is taking off, it might have increased in value to $10 million and you'll need money to triple or quadruple your staff and to upgrade the services you offer. At this point, a 10 percent stake would cost at least $1 million.

If things continue at that pace, by the time you reach Series C funding your company might be valued at $150 million; you're going to need to put together a top-notch management team including some heavy hitters, such as a CEO, a CFO, and a VP of marketing. This is the point when you're going to need money to put together marketing partnerships and to finance a national advertising campaign. This is *real* money and the people who can provide it are the venture capital firms.

Whether you're in Series A, B, or C, here are some important things to know when dealing with early investors:

▷ **Make sure you can get along with them.** Early investors will probably own a good-sized chunk of your company and they'll probably want to have seats on your board. This means you'll be spending a lot of time with them, so how you get along on a business as well as a personal level is as important as the investor's financial resources.

▷ **Don't always go for the best financial deal.** In the early stages of getting pre-IPO funding for Amazon.com, Jeff Bezos had a lot of venture capital (VC) firms offering him money in exchange for a percentage of the company. One of those firms, Kleiner Perkins (KP), led by John Doerr, made an offer that was not the most attractive—at least financially. But Doerr offered something the other VC firms didn't: mentoring, connections, and recruiting help. "More than the money I give you," Doerr told Jeff, "I can help you win the category."

In the end, Jeff opted for the intangibles and went with Kleiner Perkins. It was a gamble that started paying off immediately. John and Jeff flew from Silicon Valley to Arkansas to woo Rick Dalzell, who became Amazon's CIO, from Wal-Mart. (Wal-Mart had one of the world's largest privately owned database systems, and getting someone with that kind of experience was essential.) They brought in Joy Covey from DigiDesign as CFO. And they brought me in, too. Doug Mackenzie, another Kleiner partner, and I are fellow Stanford alums. None of us would have come to work for Amazon if it hadn't been for the Kleiner Perkins connections. Jeff could, of course, have hired some top executive talent by using a headhunter. But the Kleiner connections gave him high-quality, pedigreed people fast. They knew exactly what kinds of people were needed to fill which slots and they streamlined the negotiation process. We didn't have to do extensive interviews or spend a lot of time on the recruiting process. People showed up at the door ready to go.

Doerr did more than help recruit key executives.

Kleiner Perkins had been early investors in Netscape and Excite@Home, and using those contacts Doerr was able to pave the way for Amazon to secure exclusive deals with all three, despite heavy competition from Barnes & Noble and others. Doerr's contacts also paved the way for Amazon's recent purchases of large stakes in Drugstore.com and HomeGrocer.com.

Now, let's be realistic. The odds are that you're not going to get John Doerr to finance your company. But if you look hard you'll probably be able to find someone like him. The key is to make sure that the venture capitalist people you're considering have connections to other key executive candidates as well as to other potential business partners. Look for a firm that knows mergers and acquisitions and, if at all possible, make sure they have Internet experience. Don't be afraid to check their references. Most important, you want strategic investor capitalists—men and women who have been there, done that. One or more of them will probably be on your board and you need to know that they'll stay involved in a way that helps you. You want to be able to go to them with pressing concerns that keep you up at night and have them help solve problems. And you want them to point out other issues that you should be worrying about.

▷ **Try to get investors off your board as quickly as possible.** The problem with having investors—especially early ones—on your board is that they don't always make decisions based on what's best for the company. Instead, they may focus on doing what's best for the short-term stock price. At first glance you'd think these two approaches are the same. But while there's plenty of overlap, they can, at times, be almost completely at odds with one another. Let me give you an example.

In July 1999, CNET announced that they'd be spending an additional $100 million over the next eighteen months on a major marketing campaign. Everyone inside the company knew that this additional advertising would be good for the company, bringing in more customers, increasing sales, and driving up revenues. But all Wall Street saw was that CNET was spending $100 million more than had been forecasted. In the month following the announcement, CNET's stock went from the mid-fifties to just under thirty. Over the next few months, as it became obvious that revenues were growing—just as the company had predicted—the stock slowly recouped its losses. CNET's board (which has many early investors) did the right thing here. But not all companies are so lucky.

It's all about taking a temporary pain for long-term gain, and you'll probably be faced with similar dilemmas sometime soon. Let's say that you want to improve your infrastructure, buy more servers, and build a more scalable site. To do so you'll have to take engineers off other projects to work on this one. During the month or two that the project is being implemented your revenues may stumble. But the improvements you make will increase revenues for several years to come. Imagine, though, that some of your investors/board members had been hoping to unload their stock during that time. They'd be doing everything possible to bump revenues up *now*, not later.

Early investors also don't like it when companies issue stock options to employees. The more stock options out there, the more diluted the investors' share and the smaller the percent of the company they own. But the fact is that you can't run an Internet company and hang on to your stars if you don't give them options.

In short, the stock market correlates with company performance in the long term but not in the short. The bottom line is that you should _not_ run your business using a model that's determined by your investors or that makes Wall Street happy for the short term. Do what's good for your business and what will help you win your category over the long haul.

If you're feeling a little overwhelmed by everything in this chapter, don't be discouraged. As a CEO or manager you're going to be dealing with money issues every day, whether you're reviewing funding for internal projects or pitching venture capitalists and angels to invest in your start-up. Knowledge, as they say, is power. And nowhere is that more true than when it comes to finances, because money has an impact on everything your company does. So if you're not completely comfortable with how to get prepared, what to say and to whom, take a few minutes and go back and reread this chapter. I know you're busy, but it'll be time well spent.

For more tips on surviving the investment jungle—and to share your own tips—visit _www.10secondmanager.com/investors._

CH@PTER 7 ## HAVE FUN!

I t's Beyond.com's quarterly meeting and I'm standing in front of the entire company; four hundred
people hanging on my every word. The past few
months have been our best ever. We put together
some major deals with publishers, added a whole
slew of new products, made huge increases in site capacity,
and had our one-millionth customer. I'm recognizing the
teams that made all these things possible when something
slams into the side of my head. It's a Nerf dart. As I turn to
see where it came from, I get hit by another. Then another. I
duck down but it's too late. I get plastered by a volley of
twenty darts.

I take the Nerf attack as a good sign. Our company is
doing well and everyone is feeling proud enough of themselves to shoot the CEO. This is corporate life at its best. Plus,
how can I complain? I'm the one who gave them the Nerf
darts in the first place. I quickly pull out my own dart gun and
fire back into the crowd.

Earlier I told you that people in Silicon Valley (and the East Coast's Silicon Alley as well) love talking about Internet time, where a second is a minute, a day is a week, a week is a month. . . . Well, the reason that little expression rings so true for so many people is that things in our world are changing incredibly quickly and people are accomplishing so much in so little time. Employees get pushed hard and expectations are high, both for the company and for ourselves.

But working hard isn't all there is to the Internet. There's also work long (spend huge amounts of time at the office and stay connected via e-mail and cell phone when you're not there); work cheap (go out of your way to dress down the office environment—no frills); work fast (stay ahead of the competition and immediately respond to customers' demands); and grow fast (hire and train new employees, implement new systems, move to new locations). This is just the way things are in the Internet world. As crazy as it may seem to people who aren't in the industry, those of us who are see the pressure and pace as completely normal.

The danger is that too many companies get so caught up in doing what they have to do that they forget one of the most important keys to Internet success: fun.

Fun? In the hard-charging, fast-changing Internet world you'd think there'd be no place (let alone time) for fun. And there's no question that sometimes that's the way it seems. But in the Internet world having fun at work is even more important than it is anywhere else. Here are just a few reasons why:

▷ While working hard, fast, cheap, and long is often a recipe for Internet success, it's also a recipe for employee burnout. Fun can extinguish burnout flames before they spread.

▷ Building a team is everything in e-commerce—more so than in any other business sector because of the focus on speed. People from different backgrounds, with different skills and different abilities all have to work together to move the company forward. Fun is often the glue that holds the members of a team together.

▷   With extremely low unemployment in the high-tech world, it's truly a sellers' job market. Jeff Bezos kept his employees tied to Amazon by giving them early stock options that vested over time. But today, competitive salaries and options are a given in most markets. What isn't a given, though, is quality of life—on the job and off—and a lot of people are choosing their employers accordingly. Fun could be the difference between keeping and losing your top performers.

Now that you know *why* you should make your workplace more fun, let's take a look at *how* to do it. Having fun will make your company—both as a business entity and as a group of individuals—healthier, stronger, and better prepared to meet the challenges you face every day and that you'll continue to face as your business grows.

🔊   **Celebrate everything.** In studies of workplace satisfaction, employees consistently say that the three things they want most and that make them happiest at work are feeling as if they're part of a team, having clearly defined goals, and getting recognition for accomplishing them. In most high-tech companies these days, the first two are easy. Employees almost always work in teams and what's expected of them is almost always clearly defined. It's the third—recognition—that too often gets neglected. Internet companies are achieving goals and breaking records all the time. As a result, success sometimes gets taken for granted.

At Beyond.com, though, we made recognizing accomplishments—even small ones—a top priority. Some managers took their teams out to lunch or for a beer after work to celebrate.

When our customer service team dug out from under a huge weekend e-mail backlog, the head of the department brought in a huge box of doughnuts and asked me to come over and say a few congratulatory words to everyone. The person who answered the most e-mails received a weekend for two in a nice hotel. And the day we handled a record number of visitors to the site, I walked up and down the hallways handing out Hershey's kisses and telling everyone what a great job the systems team had done.

Sometimes Beyond.com celebrates its accomplishments in a slightly more formal way, at Friday afternoon Splashes. These gatherings are completely optional, but about a quarter of the staff shows up every week, partly because there's always some kind of wacky contest: best tattoo, juggling, animal noises, most double-jointed, who can eat ten saltine crackers the fastest . . . These activities bring people from different departments together and build camaraderie.

I often toasted the top five achievements of the week (as determined by audience nomination). I'd get the people who should be recognized up in front of the company, tell everyone what they did, and give them all Nerf basketballs or gift certificates to the movies or something else. When the business development people put together a joint-marketing agreement with a major service provider, I gave them all lottery tickets. When we added peripherals and games to the site, everyone on that team got a video game. And the folks who negotiated a major government contract got a case of Kudos chocolate bars.

While these gifts aren't expensive, they are still very significant ways of showing recognition. People don't need to get a brand-new BMW as a reward for a job well done (although it probably wouldn't hurt). What they really want is to know that someone noticed what they did and appreciates it. And they want their coworkers to know it, too. Sometimes all it takes is sending an e-mail to an employee's coworkers and supervisors letting them know what a great job he or she is doing.

Taking someone aside, privately congratulating him or her on a job well done, and giving a $25 savings bond is fine. But it's not enough. To be most effective, celebrations have to be genuine, spontaneous, and public.

Not every celebration, of course, can be spontaneous (although they're *always* genuine and public). Beyond.com celebrated its biggest achievements in a more memorable way, at monthly or quarterly meetings. It's there that I'd publicly recognize the teams or individuals who improved our search efficiency from 70 to 80 percent, or who doubled our scaling capacity, or cut the time it takes us to process a customer's order from 45 to 25 seconds.

Beyond.com also made a point of celebrating major corporate milestones that *everyone* had contributed to, such as processing the millionth digital download or passing $100 million in total revenue. When we recorded the millionth customer we had a random drawing for a trip to someplace that's a million feet from the office (a ski trip to Tahoe). For the second millionth customer, the lucky winner was scheduled to go two million feet—somewhere near Los Angeles.

What you'll discover is that it's just as much fun—and as satisfying—to be the one who's giving the awards as it is to receive them.

2. **Get out of your ivory tower.** The Internet world is the antithesis of the traditional, white-collar workplace hierarchy where everyone kowtows to the people in the management layers above them. Here, the structure is much more horizontal. Everyone owns the company and has a big stake in its future. Everyone contributes to its success in a significant way, and everyone is capable of bringing the entire site down.

Nevertheless, there's still plenty of misplaced respect in most companies: too many people revere the CEO or their supervisor just because he or she occupies a particular position. Now, respect is generally a good thing, but when it starts stifling creativity and interpersonal relationships, it's not. You simply can't be an imperious CEO or manager and be effective. So it's up to you to break down the hierarchy.

One simple way to do this is to keep a candy jar on your desk. This may sound like a minor detail, but it really worked to remove some of the layers. Everyone who came into my office at Beyond.com helped him- or herself to whatever was in the jar (I like candy corn, but my assistant, Bonnie, usually stocked the jar with Red Hot Fireballs or took requests from others). It's sort of like offering tea or coffee to a guest: even the quickest interactions seem more casual and relaxed. And I really loved that people (and there were a lot of them) felt comfortable enough to sneak into my office when I wasn't there and raid my jar.

3.   Show 'em how to have fun. No matter what managers say or what kind of candy they have in their candy jars, the best way to flatten the corporate structure is to set an example of the kind of behavior that's okay. One of my favorite ways to do this at Beyond.com was getting together with a bunch of employees to play basketball in the outdoor parking lot. We would play two-on-two in all sorts of combinations: old vs. young, new hires vs. seasoned vets, execs vs. anyone else. The parking lot was usually full and there were always people driving through looking for spaces. The ball was always getting loose and bouncing off parked cars and setting off their alarms. It was a blast. Best of all, though, it reinforced the idea that having fun is not just something management talks about; it's also something we support and actively encourage.

Another great way to demonstrate the company's commitment to fun is to not be afraid to make yourself look like a fool. At Beyond.com, I had what I called my CEO Cart, which I pushed around the office on common holidays. For Independence Day, for example, I dressed up as Uncle Sam—complete with beard and tall hat—and wandered around the office, handing out little American flags to everyone I saw while the boom box on my cart blasted the "Star-Spangled Banner." I dressed up as a groundhog on Groundhog Day and as Abe Lincoln (I guess I have a thing for beards and hats) on Presidents' Day.

Doing this serves several important purposes. It shakes up the routine and gives people a short but usually well-deserved break. It also gives me a chance to shake everyone's hand and wish them a good weekend. Most important, though, seeing that I have fun myself and that I'm perfectly willing to look ridiculous gives everyone else in the company explicit "permission" to have fun themselves.

I have to admit that my motives in all of this weren't always 100 percent altruistic. Managers can burn out just like anyone else. It's exhausting having to travel all the time, it's exhausting running a business in a constantly changing environment, and it's especially exhausting having to be "on" all the time—you've got to maintain a positive attitude for your investors, your employees, and the press. Having a little fun around the office can give you a rare and very welcome chance to relax.

4. **Encourage individual expression.** In a fast-growing, hard-working company, it's not all that uncommon to have never met the people who work two or three offices or cubicles away. Sounds strange, but it's true. In February of 1999, Snowball.com had 37 employees; by December, they were up over 250. There's no way that all those people could have gotten to know one another. For that reason, Beyond.com employees are encouraged to personalize their work spaces with toys, games, posters, artwork, or anything else. The same goes for the outside of their offices. Having interesting stuff (funny pictures, memorable quotes, and especially something about non-work-related hobbies or passions) posted outside offices promotes interaction and familiarity.

An important part of encouraging individual expression is to get rid of the dress code. In fact, if you wander the halls of most Silicon Valley companies you'll probably see a lot of longhaired, unshaven people wearing torn jeans or baggy shorts. And that's just the executives.

Not having a dress code is an important part of "fun-ifying" the corporate culture. It's also a clear statement about the importance of substance over form. Are you getting your job done? Are the customers happy? If so, who cares what you wear or whether you have a tongue ring. After all, you're going to be spending a lot of your time at the office; and you're going to be in those clothes for a long, long time, so you might as well be comfortable. (I do, though, keep a shirt and a tie at the office just in case I get called away to an urgent meeting or media event.)

Another great reason for junking the dress code is that it can make your truly formal occasions a lot more fun. See-ing people who usually wear shorts dressed in tuxes or ball gowns at the Beyond.com holiday party was more fun than Halloween.

5.   **Encourage team expression.** In the Internet world—just like in the traditional business world—there are natural rivalries between departments: marketing vs. engineering, sales vs. editorial, and so on. But in the Internet world—far more than in the traditional business world—people from different departments often have to work closely with one another on specific projects. These ad-hoc, cross-department teams form and have to get up to speed quickly. And the better everyone knows one another the faster this happens.

Beyond.com offers a lot of opportunities for people to min-gle interdepartmentally—the Friday Splashes being just one. Another great way to bring people from different departments together is to encourage each department to let the rest of the company know who they are and what they do. At Sparks.com each department has its own bulletin board where they post news and information for everyone to see. At Beyond, we gave every department a $500 budget to create a group identity. Members of one of the teams walked around the building wearing cones and they hung handheld games and toys from the ceiling in their area. Another team had an "X-Files" theme and yet another featured the "Simpsons." People from other departments were curious about the craziness going on in another part of the building and they would head over to take a look. It was fun, it got people together, and talking.

6. Integrate fun into your corporate identity. Employees' work environments and wardrobes shouldn't be the only fun things in your building. At Beyond.com you couldn't walk twenty feet down any hallway without coming across a Nerf dart gun. Crossword puzzles hung on the coffee room walls and anyone who wanted to could contribute an answer or two. Ping-Pong and air hockey and foosball tables helped people burn off steam and promoted socializing. Random employees posted "two truths and a lie" about themselves up on a white board and employees guessed which was the lie.

We converted a few Beyond.com meeting rooms into game rooms. It was a great comfort knowing there was a whole room filled with toys—anything from squirt guns to Etch-a-Sketch—and that you could go in and play at any time. It was a great employee draw and an even better way to get families together when they visited for open houses.

Plenty of other Internet companies have made having fun a part of their corporate personality. At Amazon the whole office had a funky, frugal-but-fun flavor. Crayon-filled drawing stations are scattered around the building and the company has come-as-your-favorite-book-character parties. Most of the desks in the building are nothing more than a door set across a pair of two-drawer file cabinets. The philosophy is to spend money only on things the customers see, like engineers to make the site run better, and servers to make it run faster. Sparks.com takes this whole desk thing even further. There, desks are made of doors set on pairs of sawhorses. Each employee gets to paint his or her door/desk any way they want. Stripes, patterns, and even hand- and footprints (made by dogs and kids tracking through the paint) abound.

At Excite@Home, the image is more young and playful. The walls are painted bright red and yellow and there are wildly detailed bicycles that the staff can ride from one end of the office to the other. Best of all, there's a red, plastic, swirling slide that people can use to get from the second floor to the first. Sparks.com has a slide, too; plus, they have an open dog policy—dog-owning employees can bring their pets to the office anytime they want.

Making fun part of your corporate culture can have other benefits as well. Traditional businesses have known this for years, taking clients out golfing or to football games and signing contracts between putts. In the Internet world the idea's the same but the games have changed. Steve Jurvetson, a partner at Draper Fisher Jurvetson, a Valley venture capital firm, plays a weekly game of Ultimate Frisbee with a group of entrepreneurs. The term sheet to finance www.Four11.com (the Internet white pages company) was signed on the trunk of a car after a game.

7. **Integrate new employees quickly.** There are lots of ways to quickly bring new employees into your corporate family. These activities work really well when your workplace is growing at a steady pace. But what if you suddenly have to integrate fifty or a hundred new people at once? With mergers and acquisitions rampant in the Internet, it's a real possibility. Here's one terrific way of handling this kind of situation.

Just after Beyond bought BuyDirect, we had a special event to bring the two teams together. We put together a list of about fifty word pairs (like salt and pepper) and taped one word on one person's back, the matching word on someone else's. Then everyone had to wander through the crowd of more than one hundred people and find their mate. One of BuyDirect's engineers hooked up with a Beyond.com marketing person to make peanut butter and jelly, and a Beyond administrative assistant sporting jam "reunited" with toast and the head of BuyDirect's customer service department. Without an event like that people from different levels and different companies would never have had a chance to meet and get to know each other.

Another conventional approach is to insist on manager/employee reviews every quarter. Force the two-way dialogue on what's working, what's not, and how things can be improved. They only have to be formal once per year, but the informal meetings are key to ongoing better communication and quick integration. The bottom line is that in this business, familiarity often breeds success.

8. **Make your company family-friendly.** A culture of fun is a culture that keeps people feeling alive and fulfilled. And as much as your employees may love their jobs, the one thing most people say adds value to their lives and gives them the greatest sense of satisfaction is their family. (Despite the prevailing image, not everyone in Silicon Valley is twenty-something and single. There are plenty of people out there who have families.) But thanks to the pressures of life on the Internet, most of these folks don't get to spend as much time with their spouses and kids as they'd like to.

There are several reasons why you should go out of your way to make your company as family-friendly as possible. One is that making people choose between their jobs and the people they love is a rotten thing to do. Another, as I mentioned, is it's a sellers' market out there; employees who don't like the nontangible benefits will take their services elsewhere.

One way to help bridge the gap between work and family is to make employees' families welcome at as many company events as possible. We invited families to most of Beyond.com's

Friday afternoon Splashes as well as to Halloween and holiday parties.

Another way to support families is to adopt the same idea about work schedules as you do about dress codes: substance is more important than form. Beyond.com supported people taking time off when they needed to and were pretty open to any employee's flex-time suggestions. My assistant, Bonnie, had her office calls forwarded to her cell phone whenever she was away from her desk. On more than one occasion I would be sitting in my office in the morning and she'd call to tell me that there was someone waiting in the lobby to see me. Not an unusual occurrence at all, except for the fact that Bonnie was driving her kids to school when she called. The receptionist in the lobby had buzzed Bonnie, who took the call from behind the wheel of her car and then called me. Hey, if she could be that efficient from her car, I'm all for it.

9. **Pursue nonoffice passions and encourage your employees to do the same.** Everyone needs time for individual fun. For me, two things count: basketball and my family. My work shouldn't get in the way of either.

Things are different in Silicon Valley than in most other places in the country. Here, companies are building workout palaces to keep their employees fit and happy. It didn't take them long to figure out that having fit employees would help lower the company's medical costs. Most employers, however, aren't quite as advanced when it comes to spiritual (in my case that means being with my family) health.

The Internet wins all battles. You get calls on the weekends, last-minute trips out of town, emergency projects that keep you at work late. It's nearly impossible to take long vacations because something will always come up to drag you back to the office. But if you plan things right, you can win the war. You may not be able to go away for two weeks at a stretch, but you can put together a half-dozen three-day weekends over the course of a year.

You don't, of course, have to have a family to get away from the office, but whether you (or your employees) do or not, it's essential that you *do* take time off. A life that's all Internet all the time is a horrible life indeed. Taking time off, though, is pretty worthless if the time isn't really *off.*

Sometimes people need a little help cutting the umbilical cord that keeps them connected to the office. That's why Candice Carpenter, CEO of iVillage, stands by the exit doors and takes laptops and cell phones away from people leaving on vacations.

10. **Go for group exhaustion.** Every once in a while a project will come up that is an absolute killer. It's huge and it has to be done yesterday and it's not going to be fun. But if you've built a culture where people know each other and are enthusiastic about working together in teams, these crushing projects can at least be *more* fun than they would be in another, less group- and fun-oriented company.

Fun doesn't necessarily mean mirth and laughter. It can be working hard and accomplishing a goal as a group. In early 1999, a number of Beyond.com's customers complained that the site was sluggish. We had to figure out why and we had to do it fast. Was it machinery? Bad code? A new feature taking up too much CPU time and slowing everything else down? We had no idea. The only solution was to dive in. Easy to say, but it meant that people who routinely put in ten to twelve hours a day had to rally together for seventy-two straight hours trying to debug the entire system. Sure, it was exhausting for everyone concerned, but it was also a blast. If all these people would have had to work on the project individually, they would have burned out quickly. Working as a group under unreasonable circumstances, the employees shared a "runner's high" from the shared exhilaration over achieving a seemingly impossible goal.

Of course I tried as much as I could to keep these killer projects to a minimum, partly because, quite often, after the project is finished, employees feel a tremendous letdown. They've been so excited and hyped up that they actually feel depressed when it's over. Felicia Lindau, the CEO of Sparks.com, has come up with a solution to this problem: work toward accomplishing a greater number of smaller milestones rather than a small number of large ones.

68. **Rotate your stars.** Part of having fun is the feeling of refreshment. Sometimes that means a break at the end of a day or spending a weekend—sans cell phone—backpacking. And sometimes it means giving people a new perspective on their job because no matter how much fun your workplace is, people can still burn out if they're doing the same thing, day in and day out for months or even years. At DoubleClick.com, CEO Kevin O'Connor has a policy that every job in the company is open to everyone, and employees are encouraged to rotate to other jobs they're qualified for. Rotation is especially important with your stars, the people who are most valuable to the company, and the ones you can least afford to have quit on you. So if at all possible, give everyone in your company a chance to explore other options and develop their skills in other areas. You—and your employees—might just learn some wonderful things about each other.

In the old days, gold watches and pensions were enough to keep people working at the same company for twenty, thirty, forty years. But in the Internet age, employees won't even stick around for two years, let alone twenty, if you don't keep them happy. They know they're in high demand and they aren't the least bit worried about losing their jobs. Managing a workforce like this is like managing a company full of volunteers: people stay because they want to; the moment they no longer feel like it, they're gone.

So think of having fun at work as a kind of employee recognition program for the instant-gratification age. It might seem odd to talk about "long-term" in the Internet world, where time is so compressed and everything is happening so quickly. But Internet companies—just like traditional ones—want and expect to be around for years and years. Having fun is one of the best possible long-term investments you can make in your company's future.

For more ideas on fun in the workplace—and to share your ideas—visit *www.10secondmanager.com/fun.*

Epilogue

The Internet is constantly moving, growing, and changing. And a book written on the Internet needs to move, grow, and change as well.

Accordingly, I invite you to visit *www.10secondmanager.com* after reading this book. There, you'll find a lively, ongoing exchange of ideas, as well as new tips from Internet industry leaders, influencers, and me on how to survive, thrive, and drive on the Internet. Come join us and add your insights to the discussion. See you there!

About the Authors

When it comes to thriving in the dot-com universe, **Mark Breier** has few peers. His experience building two of the Web's top ten sites—Beyond.com and Amazon.com—as well as two leading bricks-and-mortar retailers—Dreyer's/Edy's Ice Cream and Kraft Foods—means that Mark understands the business from both sides of the digital divide. Currently, Mark is one of Silicon Valley's hottest e-commerce consultants.

Mark's co-author, **Armin A. Brott,** is an MBA with a somewhat unusual résumé. An ex-commodities trader (and ex-Marine), he is the author of several best-selling books. He lives in Berkeley, California, with his two children.